# IELTS Academic

Practice Tests 1–3

Andrew Betsis | Lawrence Mamas

INNOVA PRESS LIMITED

# Introduction

**IELTS** is the International English Language Testing System. It tests all four language skills: Listening, Reading, Writing and Speaking. It is intended for people who want to study or work in an English-speaking country.

There are **two** versions of the test, the **Academic** module and the **General Training** module. The Academic module is for those who want to study or train in an English-speaking university. University admission to undergraduate and postgraduate courses is based on the results of the Academic test. The General Training module is mainly for those who are going to English-speaking countries to do secondary education or get a job; it focuses on basic survival skills in social and workplace environments.

All candidates have to take the Listening & Speaking Modules. There are different versions for the Reading and the Writing Modules, depending on whether candidates are taking the Academic or the General Training module of the test.

## IELTS FORMAT

### Academic
For entry to undergraduate or postgraduate studies or for professional reasons.

### General Training
For entry to vocational or training programmes not at degree level, for admission to secondary school and for immigration purposes.

**IELTS** is scored on a **9-band scale**. Candidates will be given a score for overall language ability, as well as another score for each of the four skills (Listening, Reading, Writing and Speaking).

### The test Modules are taken in the following order:

| MODULE | QUESTIONS | TIME | QUESTION TYPES |
|---|---|---|---|
| **Listening** | 4 sections, 40 items | approximately 30 minutes | multiple choice, short-answer questions, sentence completion, notes, form completion, table, summary, flow-chart completion, labelling a diagram/map/plan, classification, matching |
| **Academic Reading** | 3 Sections, 40 items | 60 minutes | multiple choice, short-answer questions, sentence completion, notes, form completion, table, summary, flow-chart completion, labelling a diagram/map/plan, classification, matching, choosing suitable paragraph headings, identification of author's views, yes, no, not given, true, false, not given questions |
| **General Training Reading** | 3 sections, 40 items | 60 minutes | |
| **Academic Writing** | 2 tasks | 60 minutes | **Task 1** (150 words – 20 minutes) Candidates have to look at a diagram, chart or graph and present the information in their own words. **Task 2** (250 words – 40 minutes) Candidates have to present a solution to a problem or present and justify an opinion. |
| **General Training Writing** | 2 tasks | 60 minutes | **Task 1** (150 words – 20 minutes) Candidates have to respond to a problem with a letter asking for information. **Task 2** (250 words – 40 minutes) Candidates have to present a solution to a problem or present and justify an opinion. |
| **Speaking** | | 11 to 14 minutes | It consists of three parts: **Part 1** – Introduction and interview **Part 2** – Long turn **Part 3** – Discussion |
| | | **Total Test Time** 2 hours 44 minutes | |

# Contents

Innova Press is an ELT publisher launched in 2017 with a mission to promote innovation in language education. We create readers, test preparation and practice materials and other titles in print and digital form based on the latest research in language education, with a specific focus on learner needs.

Published by Innova Press Ltd.
Suite 1, 3rd Floor, 11–12 St James's Square
London SW1Y 4LB
United Kingdom

ISBN 978-1-78768-037-1

British Library Cataloguing-in-Publication Data
A catalogue record for this book is available from the British Library.

Project management: Richard Peacock
Production and design: Global Blended Learning Ltd
Cover design: Becky Holland & Partners (BH&P)
Editorial: Sarah MacBurnie
Audio recording: Global ELT recordings; Wired Studios Ltd.

This edition is not for sale in the following territories:

| | |
|---|---|
| Australia | Italy |
| Canada | New Zealand |
| Cyprus | Romania |
| France | Spain |
| Greece | Taiwan |
| Hungary | UK |
| Ireland | USA |

## Listening

**SECTION 1   Questions 1–10**

**Questions 1–7**

*Complete the form below.*

*Write **NO MORE THAN THREE WORDS AND/OR A NUMBER** for each answer.*

### Details of Order

| | |
|---|---|
| **Party Host** | **Example:** Customer's *eldest daughter* |
| **Occasion** | 18th birthday |
| **Number of Guests Invited** | 1 ..................................... |
| **Customer Budget** | 2 *maximum* ..................................... £800 |
| **Marquee Size** | 3 ..................................... X 9 metres |
| 4 ..................................... **Cost** | £450 |
| 5 ..................................... | £150 |
| **Lighting Cost** | approximately 6 £..................................... |
| **Number of Guests** | seated 30/standing 50 |
| **Furniture Cost** | per table £4.00/per chair £3.00 |
| **Dates Marquee Required** | set-up date 7 ..................................... |
| | to be taken down on June 7th |

**Questions 8–10**

*Complete the form below.*

*Write **NO MORE THAN TWO WORDS AND/OR A NUMBER** for each answer.*

### Customer Details

| | |
|---|---|
| **First Name & Surname:** | 8 ..................................... |
| **Postcode:** | 9 ..................................... |
| **Contact Number:** | 10 ..................................... |

## SECTION 2　Questions 11–20

### Questions 11–15

*Label the map below of a typical medieval castle.*

*Write the correct letter, A–G, next to questions 11–15.*

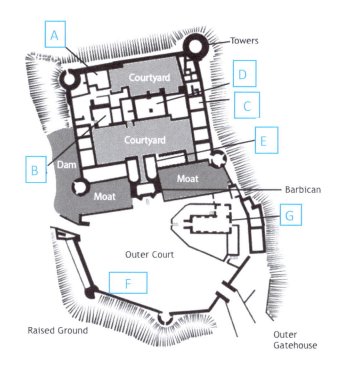

| 11 | Chapel | .......... |
| 12 | Great Hall | .......... |
| 13 | Great Chambers | .......... |
| 14 | Bakehouse | .......... |
| 15 | Stables | .......... |

### Questions 16–20

*Choose the correct letter, A, B or C.*

16　Medieval castles

　A　shared a common design.

　B　were each unique.

　C　had the same methods of fortification in common.

17　The early medieval keep served as

　A　a prison and fortified tower.

　B　a fortified tower and living area.

　C　extra storage space.

18　In later medieval castles, the keep

　A　evolved into a set of different buildings.

　B　was no longer used.

　C　played a less significant role in the castle's domestic life.

19　The term 'dungeon'

　A　was used for prisons that weren't above ground.

　B　was not used by the French.

　C　was the early name for a castle.

20　The least effective line of defence was

　A　the portcullis.

　B　the drawbridge.

　C　the barbican.

## SECTION 3   Questions 21–30

### Questions 21–25

*Choose the correct letter, A, B or C.*

21  Julie thought the lecture

    A   was just like all the others she has been to.

    B   looked at the topic in an interesting way.

    C   proved that Shakespeare had seen a ghost.

22  Hamlet was a play

    A   that was originally written in Danish.

    B   that recorded historical events.

    C   that was influenced by both English and Danish beliefs.

23  In the time of James I,

    A   a belief in ghosts was not tolerated.

    B   no one believed in ghosts.

    C   certain religious beliefs were not acceptable.

24  Shakespeare introduced ghosts into plays

    A   because he believed in a spirit world.

    B   as a theatrical device.

    C   to encourage people to change their religion.

25  Shakespeare's audience would probably have

    A   secretly approved of a supernatural content in plays.

    B   shown approval for plays with a supernatural content.

    C   disapproved of the inclusion of ghosts in plays.

### Questions 26–30

*What does Julie think about the following subjects?*

*Write the correct letter, A, B or C, next to questions 26–30.*

| A | disapproving/disbelieving |
| --- | --- |
| B | open-minded |
| C | believing |

| 26 | witches/astrology | ....... |
| --- | --- | --- |
| 27 | ghosts | ....... |
| 28 | UFOs/aliens | ....... |
| 29 | premonitions | ....... |
| 30 | telepathy | ....... |

## SECTION 4   Questions 31–40

### Questions 31–35

*Complete the notes below.*

*Write **NO MORE THAN THREE WORDS** for each answer.*

> Darwin is credited with having single-handedly changed our understanding of the
>
> 31 ................................. . However, Alfred Russell Wallace, simultaneously came up with an
>
> 32 ................................. to Darwin's. Unfortunately for Wallace, Darwin seems to have been
>
> given the 33 ................................. for the theory of evolution. Darwin's theory was very
>
> 34 ................................. and upset the religious authorities, which held very different views at
>
> that time. Today, it is generally accepted that Man is a product 35 ................................. and
>
> not spontaneous creation.

### Questions 36–40

*Complete the sentences below.*

*Write **NO MORE THAN TWO WORDS** for each answer.*

36  The absence of a ................................. might be seen by some to discredit Darwin's theory.

37  Finding an evolutionary bridge between Man and ape would provide undeniable .......................... ..................... the theory of evolution.

38  In fact, the hoax proved ................................. that scientists and the Press alike believed it was true.

39  After 40 years, Piltdown Man was declared as being no more than ................................. .

40  Even today, questions ................................. about the link between ape and man.

Practice Test 1

# Reading

## SECTION 1    Questions 1–13

*Read the text below and answer Questions 1–13.*

### Albert Einstein

Albert Einstein is perhaps the best-known scientist of the 20th century. He received the Nobel Prize for Physics in 1921, and his theories of special and general relativity are of great importance to many branches of physics and astronomy. He is well known for his theories about light, matter, gravity, space and time. His most famous idea is that energy and mass are different forms of the same thing.

Einstein was born in Württemberg, Germany, on 14th March, 1879. His family was Jewish but he was not very religious in his youth, although he became very interested in Judaism in later life.

It is well documented that Einstein did not begin speaking until after the age of three. In fact, he found speaking so difficult that his family was worried that he would never start to speak. When Einstein was four years old, his father gave him a magnetic compass. It was this compass that inspired him to explore the world of science. He wanted to understand why the needle always pointed north whichever way he turned the compass. It looked as if the needle was moving itself. But the needle was inside a closed case, so no other force (such as the wind) could have been moving it. This is how Einstein became interested in studying science and mathematics.

In fact, he was so clever that at the age of 12 he taught himself Euclidean geometry. At 15, he went to school in Munich, which he found very boring. He finished secondary school in Aarau, Switzerland, and entered the Swiss Federal Institute of Technology in Zürich, from which he graduated in 1900. But Einstein did not like the teaching there either. He often missed classes and used the time to study physics on his own or to play the violin instead. However, he was able to pass his examinations by studying the notes of a classmate. His teachers did not have a good opinion of him and refused to recommend him for a university position. So, he got a job in a patent office in Switzerland. While he was working there, he wrote the papers that first made him famous as a great scientist.

Einstein had two severely disabled children with his first wife, Mileva. His daughter (whose name we do not know) was born about a year before their marriage in January 1902. She was looked after by her Serbian grandparents until she died at the age of two. It is generally believed that she died from scarlet fever, but there are those who believe that she may have suffered from a disorder known as Down Syndrome. There is not enough evidence to know for sure. In fact, no one even knew that she had existed until Einstein's granddaughter found 54 love letters that Einstein and Mileva had written to each other between 1897 and 1903. She found these letters inside a shoe box in their attic in California. Einstein and Mileva's son, Eduard, was diagnosed with schizophrenia. He spent decades in hospitals and died in Zurich in 1965.

Just before the start of World War I, Einstein moved back to Germany and became director of a school there. But in 1933, following death threats from the Nazis, he moved to the United States, where he died on 18th April, 1955.

## Questions 1–8

*Do the following statements agree with the information given in the text? For questions 1–8, write*

> **TRUE** if the statement agrees with the information
>
> **FALSE** if the statement contradicts the information
>
> **NOT GIVEN** if there is no information on this

1   The general theory of relativity is a very important theory in modern physics. ............... *Not given*

2   Einstein had such difficulty with language that those around him thought he would never learn how to speak. ............... *T*

3   It seemed to Einstein that nothing could be pushing the needle of the compass around except the wind. ............... *T*

4   Einstein enjoyed the teaching methods in Switzerland. ............... *F*

5   Einstein taught himself how to play the violin. ............... *T*

6   His daughter died of schizophrenia when she was two. ............... *F*

7   The existence of a daughter only became known to the world between 1897 and 1903. ............... *T*

8   In 1933, Einstein officially became an American citizen. ............... *T*

## Questions 9–10

*Complete the sentences below. Choose **NO MORE THAN THREE WORDS** from the text for each answer.*

> 9   He tried hard to understand how the needle could seem to move itself so that it always ........................................ .
>
> 10  He often did not go to classes and used the time to study physics ........................................ or to play music.

## Questions 11–13

*Choose the correct letter, A, B, C or D.*

11  The name of Einstein's daughter

    A   was not chosen by him.
    B   is a mystery.
    C   is shared by his granddaughter.
    D   was discovered in a shoe box.

12  His teachers would not recommend him for a university position because

    A   they did not think highly of him.
    B   they thought he was a Nazi.
    C   his wife was Serbian.
    D   he seldom skipped classes.

13  The famous physicist Albert Einstein was of

    A   Swiss origin.
    B   Jewish origin.
    C   American origin.
    D   Austrian origin.

## SECTION 2   Questions 14–26

*Read the text below and answer Questions 14–26.*

# Drinking filtered water

**A**   The body is made up mainly of water. This means that the quality of water that we drink every day has an important effect on our health. Filtered water is healthier than tap water and some bottled water. This is because it is free of contaminants; that is, of substances that make it dirty or harmful. Substances that settle on the bottom of a glass of tap water and microorganisms that carry diseases (known as bacteria or germs) are examples of contaminants. Filtered water is also free of poisonous metals and chemicals that are common in tap water and even in some bottled water brands.

**B**   The authorities know that normal tap water is full of contaminants and they use chemicals such as chlorine and bromine in order to disinfect it. But such chemicals are hardly safe. Indeed, their use in water is associated with many different conditions, and they are particularly dangerous for children and pregnant women. For example, consuming bromine for a long time may result in low blood pressure, which may then bring about unsteadiness, dizziness or fainting. Filtered water is typically free of such water disinfectant chemicals.

**C**   Filtered water is also free of metals such as mercury and lead. Mercury has ended up in our drinking water mainly because the dental mixtures used by dentists have not been disposed of safely for a long time. Scientists believe there could be a connection between mercury in the water and many allergies and cancers, as well as disorders such as ADD, OCD, autism and depression.

**D**   Lead, on the other hand, typically finds its way into our drinking water due to lead pipes. Of course, modern pipes are not made of lead, but pipes in old houses usually are. Lead is a well-known carcinogen and is associated with pregnancy problems and birth defects. This is another reason why children and pregnant women must drink filtered water.

**E**   The benefits of drinking water are well known. We all know, for example, that it helps to detoxify the body. So, the purer the water we drink, the easier it is for the body to rid itself of toxins. The result of drinking filtered water is that the body does not have to use as much of its energy on detoxification as it would when drinking unfiltered water. This means that drinking filtered water is good for our health in general. That is because the body can perform all of its functions much more easily, and this results in improved metabolism, better weight management, improved joint lubrication as well as efficient skin hydration.

**F**   There are many different ways to filter water, and each type of filter targets different contaminants. For example, activated carbon water filters are very good at taking chlorine out. Ozone water filters, on the other hand, are particularly effective at removing germs.

**G**   For this reason, it is very important to know exactly what is in the water that we drink so that we can decide what type of water filter to use. A Consumer Confidence Report (CCR) should be useful for this purpose. This is a certificate that is issued by public water suppliers every year listing the contaminants present in the water. If you know what these contaminants are, then it is easier to decide which type of water filter to get.

## Questions 14–20

*The text has seven paragraphs, **A–G**. Which paragraph contains the following information?*

*Write the correct letter, **A–G**, next to questions **14–20**.*

| | | |
|---|---|---|
| **14** | a short summary of the main points of the text | **14** .......... |
| **15** | a variety of methods used for water filtration | **15** .......... |
| **16** | making it easier for the body to get rid of dangerous chemicals | **16** .......... |
| **17** | finding out which contaminants your water filter should target | **17** .......... |
| **18** | allergies caused by dangerous metals | **18** .......... |
| **19** | a dangerous metal found in the plumbing of old buildings | **19** .......... |
| **20** | chemicals that destroy bacteria | **20** .......... |

## Questions 21–26

*Do the following statements agree with the information given in the text?*
*For questions **21–26**, write*

> **TRUE** if the statement agrees with the information
>
> **FALSE** if the statement contradicts the information
>
> **NOT GIVEN** if there is no information on this

*detoxify*

21 The type of water you consume on a regular basis has a serious impact on your overall health and wellness. .......... *T*

22 Filtered water typically contains water disinfectant chemicals. .......... *F*

23 Exposure to disinfectant chemicals may be linked to a drop in blood pressure. .......... *T*

24 Drinking tap water helps minimise your exposure to harmful elements. .......... *F*

25 People wearing artificial teeth are more likely to be contaminated. .......... *T*

26 People who are depressed often suffer from dehydration. .......... *F*

**Practice Test 1**

**SECTION 3   Questions 27–40**

*Read the text below and answer Questions 27–40.*

# Speech dysfluency and popular fillers

A speech dysfluency is any of various breaks, irregularities or sound-filled pauses that we make when we are speaking, which are commonly known as fillers. These include words and sentences that are not finished, repeated phrases or syllables, instances of speakers correcting their own mistakes as they speak and "words" such as 'huh', 'uh', 'erm', 'um', 'hmm', 'err', 'like', 'you know' and 'well'.

Fillers are parts of speech which are not generally recognised as meaningful, and they include speech problems, such as stuttering (repeating the first consonant of some words). Fillers are normally avoided on television and films, but they occur quite regularly in everyday conversation, sometimes making up more than 20% of "words" in speech. But they can also be used as a pause for thought.

Research in linguistics has shown that fillers change across cultures and that even the different English-speaking nations use different fillers. For example, Americans use pauses such as 'um' or 'em', whereas the British say 'uh' or 'eh'. Spanish speakers say 'ehhh', and in Latin America, where they also speak Spanish, 'este' is used (normally meaning 'this').

Recent linguistic research has suggested that the use of 'uh' and 'um' in English is connected to the speaker's mental and emotional state. For example, while pausing to say 'uh' or 'um' the brain may be planning the use of future words. According to the University of Pennsylvania linguist Mark Liberman, 'um' generally comes before a longer or more important pause than 'uh'. At least that's what he used to think.

Liberman has discovered that as Americans get older, they use 'uh' more than 'um' and that men use 'uh' more than women, no matter their age. But the opposite is true of 'um'. The young say 'um' more often than the old, and women say 'um' more often than men at every age. This was an unexpected result because scientists used to think that fillers had to do more with the amount of time a speaker pauses for, rather than with who the speaker was.

Liberman mentioned his finding to fellow linguists in the Netherlands and this encouraged the group to look for a pattern outside American English. They studied British and Scottish English, German, Danish, Dutch and Norwegian, and found that women and younger people said 'um' more than 'uh' in those languages as well.

Their conclusion was that it is simply a case of language change in progress and that women and younger people are leading the change. And there is nothing strange about this. Women and young people normally are the typical pioneers of most language change. What is strange, however, is that 'um' is replacing 'uh' across at least two continents and five Germanic languages. Now this really is a mystery.

The University of Edinburgh sociolinguist Josef Fruehwald may have an answer. In his view, 'um' and 'uh' are pretty much equivalent. The fact that young people and women prefer the former is not significant. This often happens in language when there are two options. People start using one more often until the other is no longer an option. It's just one of those things.

As to how such a trend might have gone from one language to another, there is a simple explanation, according to Fruehwald. English is probably influencing the other languages. We all know that in many countries languages are constantly borrowing words and expressions of English into their own language, so why not borrow fillers, too? Of course, we don't know for a fact whether that's actually what's happening with 'um', but it is a likely story.

## Questions 27–34

*Do the following statements agree with the information given in the text? For questions 27–34, write*

> **TRUE** if the statement agrees with the information
>
> **FALSE** if the statement contradicts the information
>
> **NOT GIVEN** if there is no information on this

27  Fillers are usually expressed as pauses and probably have no linguistic meaning although they may have a purpose.
...................... *T*

28  In general, fillers vary across cultures.
...................... *T*

29  Fillers are uncommon in everyday language.
...................... *F*

30  American men use 'uh' more than American women do.
...................... *F*

31  Younger Spaniards say 'ehhh' more often than older Spaniards.
...................... *T*

32  In the past, linguists did not think that fillers were about the amount of time a speaker hesitates.
...................... *T*

33  During a coffee break, Liberman was chatting with a small group of researchers.
...................... *T*

34  Fruehwald believes that age and gender differences are significantly related to the use of 'um' and 'uh'.
...................... *F*

## Questions 35–40

*Choose the correct letter, A, B, C or D.*

35  Fillers are not

    A  used to give the speaker time to think.

    B  phrases that are restated.

    C  used across cultures.

    D  popular with the media.

36  It had originally seemed to Mark Liberman that

    A  'um' was followed by a less significant pause than 'uh'.

    B  'uh' was followed by a shorter pause than 'um'.

    C  'uh' was followed by a longer pause than 'um'.

    D  the use of 'um' meant the speaker was sensitive.

37  Contrary to what linguists used to think, it is now believed that the choice of filler

    A  may have led to disagreements.

    B  depends on the characteristics of the speaker.

    C  has nothing to do with gender.

    D  only matters to older people.

38  According to Liberman, it's still a puzzle why

    A  a specific language change is so widely spread.

    B  the two fillers are comparable.

    C  we have two options.

    D  'um' is preferred by women and young people.

39  Concerning the normal changes that all languages go through as time goes by,

    A  old men are impossible to teach.

    B  men tend to lead the way.

    C  young men simply copy the speech of young women.

    D  women play a more important role than men.

40  According to Fruehwald, the fact that 'um' is used more than 'uh'

    A  proves that 'um' is less important.

    B  shows that young people have low standards.

    C  shows that they have different meanings.

    D  is just a coincidence.

# Writing

## WRITING TASK 1

*You should spend about 20 minutes on this task.*

Below is a graph showing the incidence of mental illness (as indicated by receipt of Incapacity Benefit) amongst older UK males from 1971–2015. The reform in the benefits system took place in 1995.

> Summarise the information by selecting and reporting the main features and make comparisons where relevant.
>
> *Write at least 150 words.*

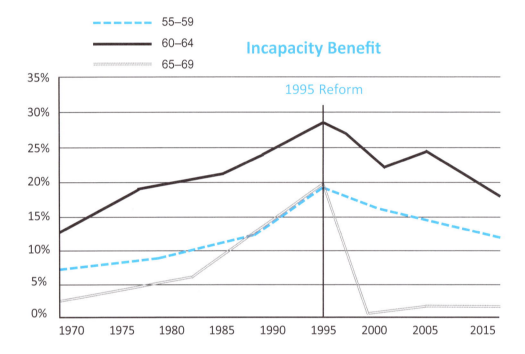

## WRITING TASK 2

*You should spend about 40 minutes on this task.*

*Write about the following topic:*

> Psychological illnesses may not be as obvious as physical disabilities or illnesses. Nevertheless, they are just as disabling in their own way. Society, however, is more accepting of those with physical than psychological illnesses or disabilities, the latter being regarded as a 'taboo' subject sometimes. To what extent do you agree with this view?

*Give reasons for your answer and include any relevant examples from your own knowledge or experience.*

*Write at least 250 words.*

# Speaking

## PART 1 *(4–5 minutes)*

The examiner will ask you some questions about yourself, your home, work or studies and other familiar topics, for example:

***Let's talk about stress and emotions.***
- *What makes you happy/sad?*
- *How do you cope with stress and negative emotions?*
- *Do you only share happy rather than sad emotions with others? Why/Why not?*
- *What emotions are more difficult for you to express?*
- *Do you think it's better to keep your emotions to yourself?*

The examiner will then ask you some questions about other topics, for example:

***Now let's talk about the importance of having a social network.***
- *What do you gain from having a good social network?*
- *Is it more difficult to make friends and form relationships today? Why/Why not?*
- *If you didn't have a good social circle of friends, what would you do?*
- *Do you think it is better to spend time building up friendships or work contacts? Why?*
- *In your opinion, do you think many problems in society today result from a breakdown in social networks?*

## PART 2 *(2 minutes)*

The examiner will give you a topic on a card like the one shown here and ask you to talk about it for one to two minutes. Before you talk, you will have one minute to think about what you are going to say. The examiner will give you some paper and a pencil so you can make notes if you want to.

> Describe a significant event in your life (good or bad) that made an impact on you.
> You should say:
> - what the event was
> - why it was such a significant event
> - how you felt at the time

The examiner may ask you one or two more questions when you have finished, for example:

- *Do significant events in your life usually impact others, too?*
- *Do you think that negative life events have a more lasting impact than positive ones?*

## PART 3 *(4–5 minutes)*

The examiner will ask you some more general questions which follow on from the topic in Part 2, for example:

- *Do people talk enough about their problems to other people?*
- *Should everyone have a personal psychologist, as many Americans do?*
- *In your opinion, is talking to a good friend better than talking to a psychologist?*
- *As a society, are we more caring than past generations? Why/Why not?*
- *Are there enough organisations to cope with individuals seeking professional help?*
- *Do you think that the problems that we face today are more serious than in the past?*
- *Are changes in lifestyles, both at home and work, a major cause of stress today?*
- *When trying to escape a stressful lifestyle, is the old saying 'a change is as good as a rest' true?*

## Listening

SECTION 1   Questions 1–10

Questions 1–10

*Complete the notes below.*

*Write **NO MORE THAN TWO WORDS** for each answer.*

| HOTELS | | | |
|---|---|---|---|
| **Name** | **Location** | **Cost** | **Notes** |
| Belvedere Gardens Hotel | Example:<br>*opposite*<br>Grimes Tower | $50 per night including<br>1 .................................<br>breakfast. | highly recommended<br>2 .................................<br>served each evening |
| Belfield Grande Hotel | On the south side of Edgeware<br>3 ................................. | $55 per night<br>($10 discount if<br>4 ............................. ) | price inclusive of<br>5 .................................<br>served in the guests'<br>6 ................................. |
| 7 .................................<br>Hotel | At the entrance to the<br>8 .................................<br>zone. | $28 weekdays and<br>$40 on weekends and<br>9 ................................. | must book well<br>10 ............................. |

## SECTION 2   Questions 11–20

## Questions 11–16

*Now look at the plan of King's Cross Station below.*

*Write the correct letter, A–H, next to questions 11–16.*

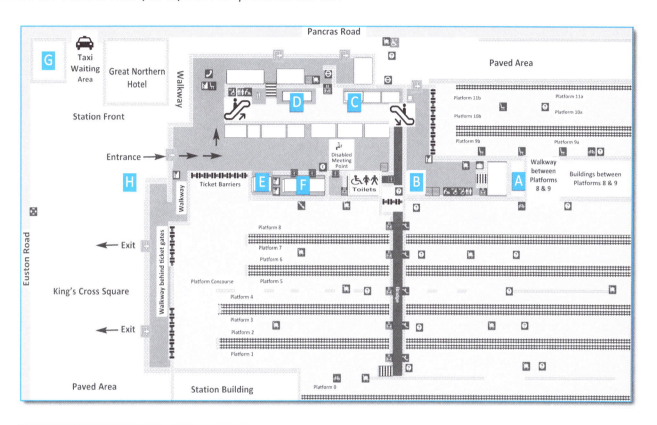

| 11 | Left Luggage Office | ................ | 14 | Ticket Office | ................ |
| 12 | Underground Station | ................ | 15 | Pizzeria | ................ |
| 13 | Burgerland | ................ | 16 | Platform 9¾ | ................ |

## Questions 17–20

*Choose the correct letter, A, B or C.*

17 The tour is going to

   A   visit all major London landmarks.

   B   only visit selected landmarks in London.

   C   visit just one of London's landmarks.

18 Tour members

   A   may be unfamiliar with the Underground.

   B   are all equally familiar with the Underground.

   C   are all unfamiliar with the Underground.

19 The tour group is intending to

   A   take a morning train.

   B   avoid trains crowded with shoppers.

   C   avoid the rush hour.

20 Seating on Underground trains

   A   has been previously reserved.

   B   can be guaranteed for those with a disability.

   C   is never guaranteed.

**Practice Test 2**

## SECTION 3   Questions 21–30
### Question 21

*Choose the correct letter, A, B or C.*

21  The construction of the new faculty building will

   A   be finished during the summer.

   B   conclude during the first term.

   C   be approved during the summer.

## Questions 22–23

*Choose two letters, A–E.*

22/23  The two main sources of funding for the project were

   A   government money.

   B   a college grant.

   C   alumni donations.

   D   the Commerce Faculty.

   E   an unnamed patron.

## Questions 24–25

*Choose two letters, A–E.*

24/25  What two new items are added to the plans?

   A   a larger gym

   B   a relaxation room

   C   a science lab

   D   a hardware zone

   E   lecture rooms

## Questions 26–30

*What does Melisa think about the following modules?*

*Write the correct letter, A, B or C, next to questions 26–30.*

| A   She will study it. | B   She won't study it. | C   She might study it. |
| --- | --- | --- |

**Modules**

| 26 | International Markets | ............... | 29 | Managing People | ............... |
| --- | --- | --- | --- | --- | --- |
| 27 | Product Placement | ............... | 30 | Public Relations | ............... |
| 28 | Organisational Behaviour | ............... | | | |

## SECTION 4    Questions 31–40
## Questions 31–32

*Complete the sentences below.*

*Write* **NO MORE THAN TWO WORDS** *for each answer.*

31  It seems that personality tests are part of our ........................................................ as they fulfil a basic human need to understand motivation.

32  Understanding why we communicate and ........................................................ others, in the way that we do, is revealed by personality tests.

## Questions 33–40

*Complete the table below.*

*Write* **NO MORE THAN THREE WORDS** *for each answer.*

| Test type | What is assessed | Who uses it | Accuracy | Advantages/ Disadvantages |
|---|---|---|---|---|
| **Graphology (Handwriting Test)** | personality based on analysis of 33 ...................... style | careers officers/ potential employers | believed to have 34 ...................... validity by the British Psychological Society | can be biased by an element of subjectivity; however, on the plus side, it is quick and easy to use |
| **Rorschach (Ink Blot Test)** | individual reactions to a series of ink blots on pieces of card | respected by 35 ...................... organisations like the Tavistock Clinic | critics regard it merely as a pseudoscience whilst others hold it in high regard | a major problem of the test is that it is affected by 36 ................... bias |
| **Luscher (Colour Test)** | individual response to 37 ...................... that are ranked in order of preference | doctors, psychologists, government agencies and universities | seemingly a 38 ...................... of psychological assessment | a benefit of the test is that it is sensitive enough to respond to individual mood changes |
| **TAT (Thematic Apperception Test)** | how an individual creates stories based on a set of cards featuring groups 39 ...................... in ambiguous scenes | those working in psychological research and forensic science | due to the 40 ...................... of a universally agreed method of scoring and standardised cards, individual comparisons are problematic | the fact that it is quick and simple to use is a huge advantage |

19

# Reading

**SECTION 1**
**Questions 1–13**

*Read the text below and answer Questions 1–13.*

## Daydreaming

Everyone daydreams sometimes. We sit or lie down, close our eyes and use our imagination to think about something that might happen in the future or could have happened in the past. Most daydreaming is pleasant. We would like the daydream to happen and we would be very happy if it did actually happen. We might daydream that we are in another person's place, or doing something that we have always wanted to do, or that other people like or admire us much more than they normally do.

Daydreams are not dreams, because we can only daydream if we are awake. Also, we choose what our daydreams will be about, which we cannot usually do with dreams. With many daydreams, we know that what we imagine is unlikely to happen. At least, if it does happen, it probably will not do so in the way we want it to. However, some daydreams are about things that are likely to happen. With these, our daydreams often help us to work out what we want to do, or how to do it to get the best results. So, these daydreams are helpful. We use our imagination to help us understand the world and other people.

Daydreams can help people to be creative. People in creative or artistic careers, such as composers, novelists and filmmakers, develop new ideas through daydreaming. This is also true of research scientists and mathematicians. In fact, Albert Einstein said that imagination is more important than knowledge, because knowledge is limited whereas imagination is not.

Research in the 1980s showed that most daydreams are about ordinary, everyday events. It also showed that over 75% of workers in so-called 'boring jobs', such as lorry drivers and security guards, spend a lot of time daydreaming in order to make their time at work more interesting. Recent research has also shown that daydreaming has a positive effect on the brain. Experiments with MRI brain scans show that the parts of the brain linked with complex problem-solving are more active during daydreaming. Researchers conclude that daydreaming is an activity in which the brain consolidates learning. In this respect, daydreaming is the same as dreaming during sleep.

Although there do seem to be many advantages of daydreaming, in many cultures it is considered a bad thing to do. One reason for this is that when you are daydreaming, you are not working. In the 19th century, for example, people who daydreamed a lot were judged to be lazy. This happened in particular when people started working in factories on assembly lines. When you work on an assembly line, all you do is one small task again and again, every time exactly the same. It is rather repetitive and, obviously, you cannot be creative. So many people decided that there was no benefit in daydreaming.

Other people have said that daydreaming leads to 'escapism' and that this is not healthy, either. Escapist people spend a lot of time living in a dream world in which they are successful and popular, instead of trying to deal with the problems they face in the real world. Such people often seem to be unhappy and are unable or unwilling to improve their daily lives. Indeed, recent studies show that people who often daydream have fewer close friends than other people. In fact, they often do not have any close friends at all.

## Questions 1–8

*Do the following statements agree with the information given in the text? For questions 1–8, write*

> **TRUE** if the statement agrees with the information
>
> **FALSE** if the statement contradicts the information
>
> **NOT GIVEN** if there is no information on this

1   People usually daydream when they are walking around.                            .....................

2   Some people can daydream when they are asleep.                                    .....................

3   Some daydreams help us to be more successful in our lives.                        .....................

4   Most lorry drivers daydream in their jobs to make them more interesting.          .....................

5   Factory workers daydream more than lorry drivers.                                 .....................

6   Daydreaming helps people to be creative.                                          .....................

7   Old people daydream more than young people.                                       .....................

8   Escapist people are generally very happy.                                         .....................

## Questions 9–10

*Complete the sentences below. Choose **NO MORE THAN THREE WORDS** from the text for each answer.*

> 9   Writers, artists and other creative people use daydreaming to .................................. .
>
> 10  The areas of the brain used in daydreaming are also used for complicated ............................. .

## Questions 11–13

*Choose the correct letter, A, B, C or D.*

11  Daydreams are

   A   dreams that we have when we fall asleep in the daytime.

   B   about things that happened that make us sad.

   C   often about things that we would like to happen.

   D   activities that only a few people are able to do.

12  In the 19th century, many people believed that daydreaming was

   A   helpful in factory work.

   B   a way of avoiding work.

   C   something that few people did.

   D   a healthy activity.

13  People who daydream a lot

   A   usually have creative jobs.

   B   are much happier than other people.

   C   are less intelligent than other people.

   D   do not have as many friends as other people.

**Practice Test 2**

## SECTION 2  Questions 14–25

*Read the text below and answer Questions 14–25.*

# Tricky sums and psychology

A    In their first years of studying mathematics at school, children all over the world usually have to learn the times tables, also known as the multiplication tables, which show what you get when you multiply numbers together. Children have traditionally learned their times tables by going from '1 times 1 is 1' all the way up to '12 times 12 is 144'.

B    Times tables have been around for a very long time now. The oldest known tables using base 10 numbers, the base that is now used everywhere in the world, are written on bamboo strips dating from 305 BCE, found in China. However, in many European cultures the times tables are named after the Ancient Greek mathematician and philosopher Pythagoras (570–495 BC). And so they are called the Table of Pythagoras in many languages, including French and Italian.

C    In 1820, in his book *The Philosophy of Arithmetic*, the mathematician John Leslie recommended that young pupils memorise the times tables up to 25×25. Nowadays, however, educators generally believe it is important for children to memorise the tables up to 9×9, 10×10 or 12×12.

D    The current aim in the UK is for school pupils to know all their times tables up to 12×12 by the age of nine. However, many people do not know them, even as adults. Recently, some politicians have been asked arithmetical questions of this kind. For example, in 1998, the schools minister Stephen Byers was asked the answer to 7×8. He got the answer wrong, saying 54 rather than 56, and everyone laughed at him.

E    In 2014, a young boy asked the UK Chancellor George Osborne the exact same question. As he had passed A-level maths and was in charge of the UK's economic policies at the time, you would expect him to know the answer. However, he simply said, 'I've made it a rule in life not to answer such questions.'

F    Why would a politician refuse to answer such a question? It is certainly true that some sums are much harder than others. Research has shown that learning and remembering sums involving 6, 7, 8 and 9 tends to be harder than remembering sums involving other numbers. It is even harder when 6, 7, 8 and 9 are multiplied by each other. Studies often find that the hardest sum is 6×8, with 7×8 not far behind. However, even though 7×8 is a relatively difficult sum, it is highly unlikely that George Osborne did not know the answer. So there must be some other reason why he refused to answer the question.

G    The answer is that Osborne was being 'put on the spot', and he didn't like it. It is well known that when there is a lot of pressure to do something right, people often have difficulty doing something that they normally find easy. When you put someone on the spot and ask such a question, it causes stress. The person's heart beats faster and their adrenalin levels go up. As a result, people will often make mistakes that they would not normally make. This is called 'choking'. Choking often happens in sport, such as when a footballer takes a crucial penalty. In the same way, the boy's question put Osborne under great pressure. He knew it would be a disaster for him if he got the answer to such a simple question wrong and feared that he might choke. That is why he refused to answer the question.

## Questions 14–20

*The text has seven paragraphs, A–G. Which paragraph contains the following information?*

*Write the correct letter, A–G, next to questions 14–19.*

| | | | |
|---|---|---|---|
| **14** | a 19th-century opinion of what children should learn | **14** | .......... |
| **15** | the most difficult sums | **15** | .......... |
| **16** | the effect of pressure on doing something | **16** | .......... |
| **17** | how children learn the times tables | **17** | .......... |
| **18** | a politician who got a sum wrong | **18** | .......... |
| **19** | a history of the times tables | **19** | .......... |

## Questions 20–25

*Do the following statements agree with the information given in the text? For questions 20–25, write*

> **TRUE** if the statement agrees with the information
>
> **FALSE** if the statement contradicts the information
>
> **NOT GIVEN** if there is no information on this

**20** Pythagoras invented the times tables in China.          ......................

**21** Stephen Byers and George Osborne were asked the same question.          ......................

**22** All children in the UK have to learn the multiplication tables.          ......................

**23** George Osborne probably did not know the answer to 7×8.          ......................

**24** 7×8 is the hardest sum that children have to learn.          ......................

**25** Stephen Byers had not been the schools minister for very long.          ......................

## SECTION 3   Questions 26–40

*Read the text below and answer Questions 26–40.*

# Care in the community

'Bedlam' is a word that has become synonymous in the English language with chaos and disorder. The term itself derives from the shortened name for a former 16th-century London institution for the mentally ill, known as St. Mary of Bethlehem. This institution was so notorious that its name was to become a byword for mayhem. Patient 'treatment' amounted to little more than legitimised abuse. Inmates were beaten and forced to live in unsanitary conditions, whilst others were placed on display to a curious public as a sideshow. There is little indication to suggest that other institutions founded at around the same time in other European countries were much better.

Even up until the mid-20th century, institutions for the mentally ill were regarded as being more places of isolation and punishment than healing and solace. In popular literature of the Victorian era which reflected true-life events, individuals were frequently sent to the 'madhouse' as a legal means of permanently disposing of an unwanted heir or spouse. Later, in the mid-20th century, institutes for the mentally ill regularly carried out invasive brain surgery known as a 'lobotomy' on violent patients without their consent. The aim was to 'calm' the patient, but ended up producing a patient who was little more than a zombie. Such a procedure is well documented to devastating effect in the film *One Flew Over the Cuckoo's Nest*. Little wonder then that the appalling catalogue of treatment of the mentally ill led to a call for change from social activists and psychologists alike.

Improvements began to be seen in institutions from the mid-50s onwards, along with the introduction of care in the community for less severely ill patients. Community care was seen as a more humane and purposeful approach to dealing with the mentally ill. Whereas institutionalised patients lived out their existence in confinement, forced to obey institutional regulations, patients in the community were free to live a relatively independent life. The patient was never left purely to their own devices, as a variety of services could theoretically be accessed by the individual. In its early stages, however, community care consisted primarily of help from the patient's extended family network. In more recent years, such care has been extended to the provision of specialist community mental health teams (CMHTs) in the UK. Such teams cover a wide range of services, from rehabilitation to home treatment and assessment. In addition, psychiatric nurses are on hand to administer prescription medication and give injections. The patient is therefore provided with the necessary help that they need to survive in the everyday world whilst maintaining a degree of autonomy.

Often, though, when a policy is put into practice, its failings become apparent. This is true for the policy of care in the community. Whilst back-up services may exist, an individual may not call upon them when needed, due to reluctance or inability to assess their own condition. As a result, such an individual may be alone during a critical phase of their illness, which could lead them to self-harm or even become a threat to other members of their community. Whilst this might be an extreme-case scenario, there is also the issue of social alienation that needs to be considered. Integration into the community may not be sufficient to allow the individual to find work, leading to poverty and isolation. Social exclusion could then cause a relapse as the individual is left to battle mental health problems alone. The solution, therefore, is to ensure that the patient is always in touch with professional helpers and not left alone to fend for themselves. It should always be remembered that whilst you can take the patient out of the institution, you can't take the institution out of the patient.

When questioned about care in the community, there seems to be a division of opinion amongst members of the public and within the mental healthcare profession itself. Dr Mayalla, a practising clinical psychologist, is inclined to believe that whilst certain patients may benefit from care in the community, the scheme isn't for everyone. 'Those suffering moderate cases of mental illness stand to gain more from care in the community than those with more pronounced mental illness. I don't think it's a one-size-fits-all policy. But I also think that there is a far better infrastructure of helpers and social workers in place now than previously, and the scheme stands a greater chance of success than in the past.'

Anita Brown, mother of three, takes a different view. 'As a mother, I'm very protective towards my children. As a result, I would not put my support behind any scheme that I felt might put my children in danger. I guess there must be assessment methods in place to ensure that dangerous individuals are not let loose amongst the public, but I'm not for it at all. I like to feel secure where I live, but more to the point, that my children are not under any threat.'

Bob Ratchett, a former mental health nurse, takes a more positive view of community care projects. 'Having worked in the field myself, I've seen how a patient can benefit from living an independent life, away from an institution. Obviously, only individuals well on their way to recovery would be suitable for consideration as participants in such a scheme. If you think about it, is it really fair to condemn an individual to a lifetime in an institution when they could be living a fairly fulfilled and independent life outside the institution?'

## Questions 26–31

*Choose the correct letter, A, B, C or D.*

26 Which of the following statements is accurate?

   A   In the 20th century, illegal surgical procedures were carried out on the mentally ill.

   B   The Victorian era saw an increase in mental illness amongst married couples.

   C   Mental institutions of the past were better equipped to deal with the mentally ill.

   D   In the past, others often benefited when a patient was sent to a mental asylum.

27 What does the writer mean by patient treatment being 'legitimised abuse'?

   A   There were proper guidelines for the punishment of mentally ill patients.

   B   Maltreatment of mentally ill patients was not illegal and so was tolerated.

   C   Only those who were legally entitled to do so could punish mentally ill patients.

   D   Physical abuse of mentally ill patients was a legal requirement of mental institutions.

28 What brought about changes in the treatment of mentally ill patients?

   A   A radio documentary exposed patient maltreatment.

   B   People rebelled against the consistent abuse of mentally ill patients.

   C   Previous treatments of mentally ill patients were proved to be ineffective.

   D   The maltreatment of mentally ill patients could never be revealed.

29 What was a feature of early care in the community schemes?

   A   Patient support was the responsibility more of relatives than professionals.

   B   Advanced professional help was available to patients.

   C   All mentally ill patients could benefit from the scheme.

   D   Patients were allowed to enjoy full independence.

30 What is true of care in the community schemes today?

   A   They are very cheap to run.

   B   More professional services are available to patients.

   C   Family support networks have become unnecessary.

   D   All patients can now become part of these schemes.

31 What can be said of the writer's attitude towards care in the community?

   A   He believes that the scheme has proved to be a failure.

   B   He believes that it can only work under certain circumstances.

   C   He believes that it will never work, as mentally ill patients will always be disadvantaged.

   D   He believes it has failed due to patient neglect by professional helpers.

## Questions 32–36

Look at the following statements, *32–36*, and the list of people below, *A–C*.

Match each statement to the correct person.

> **A**   Dr Mayalla
>
> **B**   Anita Brown
>
> **C**   Bob Ratchett

> **32**   This person acknowledges certain inadequacies in the concept of care in the community, but recognises that attempts have been made to improve on existing schemes.                                              ................
>
> **33**   This person, whilst emphasising the benefits to the patient from care in the community schemes, is critical of traditional care methods.                                              ................
>
> **34**   This person's views have been moderated by their professional contact with the mentally ill.                                              ................
>
> **35**   This person places the welfare of others above that of the mentally ill.                                              ................
>
> **36**   This person acknowledges that a mistrust of care in the community schemes may be unfounded.                                              ................

## Questions 37–40

Do the following statements agree with the information given in the text? For questions *37–40*, write

> **TRUE** if the statement agrees with the information
>
> **FALSE** if the statement contradicts the information
>
> **NOT GIVEN** if there is no information on this

**37**   Doctors are being retrained to help children with mental health issues.          ......................

**38**   Community care schemes do not provide adequate support for patients.          ......................

**39**   Dr Mayalla believes that the scheme is less successful than in the past.          ......................

**40**   The goal of community care schemes is to make patients less dependent on the system.          ......................

# Writing

## WRITING TASK 1

*You should spend about 20 minutes on this task.*

The graph below shows relative rates of language acquisition according to different study methods.

> Summarise the information by selecting and reporting the main features and make comparisons where relevant.
>
> *Write at least 150 words.*

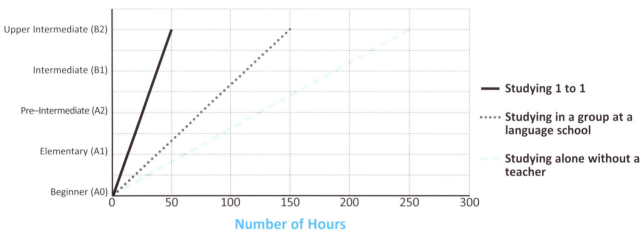

**Speed of Language Learning**

## WRITING TASK 2

*You should spend about 40 minutes on this task.*

*Write about the following topic:*

> Parents are often over-anxious to teach their children to speak. If children are 'slow developers', parents will often allow psychologists and schools to intervene and give their children speech therapy. Do you think children develop at different rates and so should be left to themselves to acquire language skills, or is such intervention justified? Discuss both views and give your own opinion.

*Give reasons for your answer and include any relevant examples from your own knowledge or experience.*

*Write at least 250 words.*

# Speaking

## PART 1 *(4–5 minutes)*

The examiner will ask you some questions about yourself, your home, work or studies and other familiar topics, for example:

- *Which skill do you find the easiest to acquire when learning a new language? Why?*
- *Do you think language skills can be learned as effectively at any age? Why/Why not?*
- *In your opinion, does learning one language make it easier to acquire others? Why/Why not?*
- *Would your life be easier if you were a 'polyglot' (someone who speaks several languages fluently)? Why/Why not?*
- *If you could choose between being fluent in English or your own language, which would you choose and why?*

The examiner will then ask you some questions about other topics, for example:

### Now let's talk about the acquisition of language skills.

- *Do you think language ability is inherited or learned? Why/Why not?*
- *In your opinion, does 'text speak' in mobile messaging teach bad language habits? Why/Why not?*
- *Should parents ensure children read books to improve their language skills? Why/Why not?*
- *In the future, will translation services like 'Google Translate' and other smartphone applications make language learning redundant? Why/Why not?*
- *Do you think that animals can acquire human language? Why/Why not?*

## PART 2 *(2 minutes)*

The examiner will give you a topic on a card like the one shown here and ask you to talk about it for one to two minutes. Before you talk, you will have one minute to think about what you are going to say. The examiner will give you some paper and a pencil so you can make notes if you want to.

> Describe a particularly memorable language lesson that you have had.
> You should say:
> - why it was so memorable
> - who gave the lesson
> - how the lesson helped you improve or focus on an aspect of language

The examiner may ask you one or two more questions when you have finished, for example:

- *Do you think 'bad' language students are just uninspired ones?*
- *How can language lessons be made more interesting and/or effective?*

## PART 3 *(4–5 minutes)*

The examiner will ask some more general questions which follow on from the topic in Part 2, for example:

- *Should 'dead languages' such as Latin and Ancient Greek be taught in schools? Why/Why not?*
- *Is more importance given to science and technology than to language learning in school?*
- *Do 'cultural exchanges' aid language acquisition? Why/Why not?*
- *Can a non-native speaker ever become as fluent as a native speaker? Why/Why not?*
- *How could language learning be taught more effectively in school?*
- *Is it worth learning a language if you are past retirement age? Why/Why not?*
- *Would it be better if everyone just learnt one universal language in school? Why/Why not?*

# Test 3

## Listening

**SECTION 1   Questions 1–10**
**Questions 1–7**

*Complete the table below.*

*Write* **NO MORE THAN THREE WORDS AND/OR A NUMBER** *for each answer.*

| Details of customer purchase | |
|---|---|
| lot number | Example: ...*2374*................... |
| reserve price | 1 £ ........................... |
| name of artist | 2 *P.J.* ........................ |
| maximum amount that could be paid | 3 £ ........................... |
| description | 4 ................. painting of a rural 5 ................ landscape |
| width of painting without frame | 6 ............................... |
| width of painting with frame | 2 metres |
| height without frame | 1 metre |
| 7 .......................... with frame | 1.5 metres |

**Questions 8–10**

*Complete the table below.*

*Write* **NO MORE THAN THREE WORDS AND/OR A NUMBER** *for each answer.*

| Customer details | |
|---|---|
| Name | Mrs   8 ................................. |
| Address | Charlton Manor, Kingston Village<br>Postcode:   9 ................................. |
| Requested delivery date | 10 ................................. (Day: Tuesday) |

## SECTION 2   Questions 11–20
## Questions 11–15

*Label the map below. Write the correct letter, A–G, next to questions 11–15.*

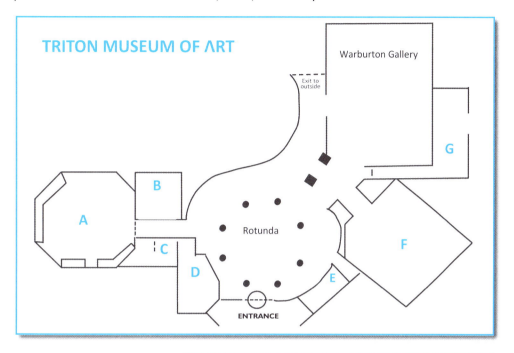

**TRITON MUSEUM OF ART**

Warburton Gallery

Exit to outside

G

B

A

Rotunda

C

D

E

F

ENTRANCE

| | | |
|---|---|---|
| **11** Cloakroom | ................ |
| **12** Permanent Collection Gallery | ................ |
| **13** Storage Room | ................ |
| **14** Cowell Room | ................ |
| **15** Staffroom Area and Kitchen | ................ |

## Questions 16–20

*Choose the correct letter, A, B or C.*

**16** All museum patrons

   **A**  receive advance information about events.

   **B**  have a discount on entry to the museum.

   **C**  can take one non-paying guest into the museum.

**17** The Masked Ball

   **A**  is an annual event.

   **B**  will be held some time in the new year.

   **C**  will be a unique event.

**18** Details of the Masked Ball

   **A**  have yet to be confirmed.

   **B**  have been finalised.

   **C**  may be provided on request.

**19** Certain events at the Garden Party are

   **A**  cheaper than others.

   **B**  liable to cancellation.

   **C**  almost fully booked.

**20** The forthcoming artistic events feature

   **A**  newcomers to the art world.

   **B**  established artists.

   **C**  a mixture of new and established artists.

**Practice Test 3**

## SECTION 3   Questions 21–30
### Questions 21–25

*Choose the correct letter, A, B or C.*

21  'Outsider' art is created by artists who

    A  lack formal art training.

    B  have a formal background in art.

    C  make a living from their work.

22  The art critic believes that

    A  the definition of 'art' is very flexible.

    B  not many people are interested in art.

    C  in theory, quality art can be produced by anyone.

23  According to the art critic, good art

    A  relies more on talent than skill.

    B  requires an equal combination of talent and skill.

    C  requires significant skill.

24  Usually the public

    A  is unimpressed by outsider art.

    B  has little knowledge of outsider artists.

    C  only appreciates unknown artists.

25  The works of Nek Chand and Ferdinand Cheval

    A  impress most due to their value.

    B  were created without official permission.

    C  were inspired by a romantic idea.

### Questions 26–30

*What does Jake say about the following?*

*Write the correct letter, A, B or C, next to questions 26–30.*

| | |
|---|---|
| A  are overrated | |
| B  lack skill | |
| C  have popular appeal | |

26  modern painters          ...............

27  outsider artists          ...............

28  Renaissance artists       ...............

29  Impressionist artists     ...............

30  modern sculptors          ...............

## SECTION 4   Questions 31–40
## Questions 31–35

*Complete the notes below.*

*Write **NO MORE THAN THREE WORDS** for each answer.*

### Animal Art

Despite the rather basic **31** ..........................................., animal paintings are impressive.

However, by **32** ........................................... standards, such artworks are considered rather primitive.

Whilst we might expect apes, our **33** ........................................... relatives, to have some artistic talent, other animal species also have artistic talent.

Recently, an interspecies exhibition of animal art was held in **34** ........................................... of such a phenomenon.

Animals, though, tend to adopt an abstract, rather than a figurative, approach to art, with the exception of that of an **35** ................................ .

## Questions 36–40

*Complete the sentences below.*

*Write **NO MORE THAN TWO WORDS** for each answer.*

**36** Today, animal artists are no longer such a ........................................... as they once were.

**37** ........................................... and tools need to be species-appropriate in order for animals to be creative.

**38** It would seem that Man and animals share ........................................... than at first thought.

**39** Some animal artworks may, however, be the result of human ........................................... .

**40** Sceptics are probably best advised, though, to keep an ........................................... when it comes to animal art.

# Reading

## SECTION 1

### Questions 1–10

*Read the text on the next page and answer Questions 1–10.*

*Complete the table below. Choose 10 answers from the box at the bottom of the page and write the correct letter, A–L, next to numbers 1–10.*

|  | Art | Craft |
|---|---|---|
| **End product** | 1 ........... | 6 ........... |
|  | 2 ........... | 7 ........... |
| **Act of creation/production** | 3 ........... | 8 ........... |
|  | 4 ........... | 9 ........... |
|  | 5 ........... | 10 ........... |

A   the finished object appeals on an emotional and spiritual level

B   the final product has no pretensions to being anything more than it appears

C   only a functional use is considered for the finished object

D   no practical purpose as such is envisaged for the created object

E   the process of creation is merely a means to an end

F   whether or not there is an end product, the product itself is secondary to the process of creation

G   not having to adhere to a set of rules, the process is a matter of experimentation

H   there is no margin of error for experimentation; all of the process following a set of guidelines

I   its goal is defined from the outset

J   the process is fluid and undefined

K   it is useful but not commercially viable

L   the production process is a mixture of following rules and experimentation

# Art or craft?

Down the centuries, craftsmen have been held to be distinct from artists. Craftsmen, such as woodworkers and plasterers, belonged to their own guild, whilst the artist was regarded as a more solitary being confined to an existence in a studio or attic. In addition, whilst craftsmen could rely on a reasonably steady income, artists were often living such a hand-to-mouth existence that the term 'starving artist' became a byword to describe the impoverished existence of artists generally. Even today, the lifestyles of the craftsman and the artist could not be more different. However, what exactly separates craft from art from both a practical and a philosophical view?

One of the main distinctions between art and craft resides in the nature of the finished product or piece. Essentially, the concept of craft is historically associated with the production of useful or practical products. Art, on the other hand, is not restricted by the confines of practicality. The craftsman's teapot or vase should normally be able to hold tea or flowers, while the artist's work is typically without utilitarian function. In fact, the very reason for art and its existence is purely to 'be', hence the fur-lined teacup created by Dada artist, Meret Oppenheim. The 'cup', as such, was quite obviously never intended for practical use any more than a chocolate teapot might have been.

Artistry in craftsmanship is therefore merely a by-product, since the primary focus is on what something does, not what it is. The reverse is true for art. Artistic products appeal purely at the level of the imagination. As the celebrated philosopher Kant stated, 'At its best, art cultivates and expands the human spirit'. Whether the artist responsible for a piece of art has sufficient talent to achieve this is another matter. The goal of all artists, nevertheless, remains the same: to produce a work that simultaneously transcends the mundane and uplifts the viewer. In contrast, the world of the craftsman and his work remain lodged firmly in the practicality of the everyday world. An object produced by an artist is therefore fundamentally different from the one produced by a craftsman.

Differences between the two disciplines of art and craft extend also to the process required to produce the finished object. The British philosopher R.G. Collingwood, who set out a list of criteria that distinguish art from craft, focused on the distinction between the two disciplines in their 'planning and execution'. With a craft, Collingwood argued, the 'result to be obtained is preconceived or thought out before being arrived at'. The craftsman, Collingwood says, 'knows what he wants to make before he makes it'. This foreknowledge, according to Collingwood, must not be vague, but precise. In fact, such planning is considered to be 'indispensable' to craft. In this respect, craft is essentially different from art. Art is placed by Collingwood at the other end of the creative continuum, the creation of art being described as a process that evolves non-deterministically. The artist is, therefore, just as unaware as anyone else as to what the end product of creation will be when he is actually in the process of creating. Contrast this with the craftsman who already knows what the end product will look like before he or she has even begun to create it.

Since the artist is not following a set of standard rules in the process of creation, he or she has no guidelines like the craftsman. Whilst the table or chair created by the craftsman, for example, has to conform to certain expectations in appearance and design, no such limitations are imposed on the artist. For it is the artist alone who, through a trial-and-error approach, will create the final object. The object merely evolves over time. Whereas the craftsman can fairly accurately predict when a product will be finished, taking technical procedures into account, the artist can do no such thing. The artist is at the mercy of inspiration alone and, quite apart from not being able to have a projected finishing date, may never be able to guarantee that the object will be finished at all. Unfinished symphonies by great composers and works of literature never completed by their authors testify to this.

Having no definite end goal in mind, the emphasis on the finished product that is true of craftsmanship is placed instead on the act of creation itself with the artist. The creation of the work of art is an exploration and a struggle and path of discovery for the artist. It could be said that the artist is producing as much for himself as for those who will view the finished product. This act of creation is very distinct from the production of an object that is crafted, therefore. The goal of making craftwork is monetary compensation. Craft is produced for purchase and is essentially a money-generating industry. Any craftsman who followed the artistic approach to creation would soon be out of a job. Craftsmen are expected to deliver, artists are not. This is probably the most fundamental difference that separates the craftsman from the artist.

## SECTION 2　Questions 11–26

*Read the text below and answer Questions 11–26.*

### Salvador Dali

Few with even a passing knowledge of the art world are likely not to have heard of Salvador Dali, the eccentric and avant-garde exponent of the Surrealist movement. Love him or loathe him, Dali's work has achieved enduring worldwide fame as his name and work have become virtually synonymous with Surrealism itself. The artist's melting clock image is surely one of the most iconic paintings of the art world, whilst Dali's antics have become the stuff of anecdote.

Born into a middle-class family in the Catalonian town of Figueres, in northeastern Spain, Dali (or Salvador Felipe Jacinto Dali Domenech, to give him his full name) aimed high from the beginning. In the artist's 1942 autobiography entitled 'The Secret Life of Salvador Dali', the artist describes how 'At the age of six I wanted to be a cook. At seven I wanted to be Napoleon. And my ambition has been growing steadily ever since.' Such ambition and self-belief matured into full-blown arrogance in later years. An example of this is amply shown on an occasion when the artist felt the examiners of the Madrid Academy he was attending were well below par.

To a degree, his undeniably impressive and precocious talent excused his conceit. He was only 14 when his first works were exhibited as part of a show in Figueres. Then, three years later, he was admitted to the Royal Academy of Fine Arts of San Fernando in Madrid. However, it wasn't long before Dali's highly developed sense of self-worth (or conceit, depending on how you view the artist) came to the fore and also affected the course of his life. Believing himself way superior to the Academy tutors, who refused to grant him a degree, the rebellious artist left for Paris. There, he hoped to avail himself of knowledge that he believed his tutors were not adequate to impart. He soon made the acquaintance of the French surrealists Jean Arp, Rene Magritte and Max Ernst, and this would prove a turning point in Dali's artistic life.

Already familiar with the psychoanalytic theories of Sigmund Freud, Dali was to witness how the French Surrealists were attempting to capture Freud's ideas in paint. The whole world of the unconscious sublimated into dreams was to become the content of these artists' work and later that of Dali's, too. International acclaim followed shortly after. In 1933, he enjoyed solo exhibitions in Paris and New York City, becoming, as one exhibition curator put it, 'Surrealism's most exotic and prominent figure'. Praise continued to be heaped on Dali as French poet and critic, Andre Breton, the leader of the Surrealist Movement, gave the artist his blessing to continue carrying the torch for the artistic movement, writing that Dali's name was 'synonymous with revelation in the most resplendent sense of the word'.

Dali's Surrealist paintings were packed with Freudian imagery: staircases, keys, dripping candles, in addition to a whole host of personally relevant symbolism, such as grasshoppers and ants, that captured his phobias on canvas. Despite Dali's overt adulation for Freud, a meeting with the grandmaster of psychoanalysis proved somewhat unfortunate. On the occasion that Dali met Freud, he proceeded to sketch the latter in earnest. However, something about Dali's fervid attitude must have alarmed the psychoanalyst, as he is said to have whispered to others in the room, 'The boy looks like a fanatic'.

Sometimes Dali not only came across as mad but also unintelligible, at least as far as his paintings were concerned. One work, 'The Persistence of Memory', was particularly singled out for the sheer confusion it caused amongst its viewers. Featuring melting clocks, swarming ants and a mollusc that was the deflated head of Dali in disguise, the images were so puzzling that one critic urged readers to 'contact Dr Freud' to uncover the meaning of the canvas. His work was, if nothing else, provocative and powerful.

With the passing years, Dali became ever more infatuated with money, admitting to a 'pure, vertical, mystical, gothic love of cash.' Accordingly, he indiscriminately endorsed a host of products for French and American TV commercials. He also never failed to promote himself and displayed increasingly exhibitionist behaviour as time went on. Most notably, he once turned up for a lecture in Paris in a Rolls Royce stuffed with cauliflowers. He obviously believed the slogan of one of his advertising campaigns for Braniff Airlines, where he declares 'When you got it, flaunt it'. As a more positive outcome of his love for money, Dali took on increasingly diverse projects, ranging from set design to designing clothes and jewellery. His critics, however, believed that early on in his career his love of money exceeded his dedication to producing great art, resulting in Dali producing 'awful junk' after 1939, according to one art critic.

Despite a lukewarm reception from critics, Dali's public popularity never declined. In 1974, at 70 years old, the Dali Theatre Museum opened in his hometown, Figueres. More of a Surrealist happening than a museum, one exhibit was a long black Cadillac that rained inside itself whenever a visitor dropped a coin into the slot. Even today, hundreds of thousands of visitors still tour the museum each year. Whatever your opinion of him, at least Dali is unlikely to ever be forgotten.

## Questions 11–13

*Complete each sentence with the correct ending, A–E, below.*

*Write the correct letter, A–E next to questions 11–13.*

11   Dali displayed a precocious talent from an early age; however, he was aware ................. .

12   Encountering the French Surrealist painters in Paris ................. .

13   Dali's artistic legacy is secure, although ................. .

A   of certain limitations in his artistic skills that became evident in his later works.

B   opened Dali's eyes to the psychoanalytic movement, the ideas of which he then incorporated into his works.

C   his artistic studies needed to be supplemented by going to Paris to meet the Surrealist artists.

D   some art critics are less impressed with his work than the general public.

E   inspired Dali to focus on the psychoanalytic content of his artwork.

## Questions 14–16

*Choose the correct letter, A, B, C or D.*

14  Dali's departure for Paris was

    **A**  inspired by a desire to learn about psychoanalysis.

    **B**  a result of being disgraced at the Madrid Academy.

    **C**  to blame for his failure to complete his Academy degree.

    **D**  a quest for self-improvement.

15  Dali came to represent the Surrealist Movement

    **A**  due to the strange poems he wrote with Breton.

    **B**  because he depicted the most memorable images of Surrealism.

    **C**  as he had a better understanding of psychoanalysis than his fellow artists.

    **D**  since he was no more talented as an artist than his peers.

16  Dali's work was

    **A**  accessible to those with an understanding of psychoanalysis.

    **B**  loaded with secret symbolism.

    **C**  more a channel for personal expression than a financial undertaking.

    **D**  to prove more popular as Dali grew older.

## Questions 17–18

*There are two correct answers. Choose two letters from A, B, C, D and E.*

17/18  What is Dali most likely to be remembered for?

    **A**  his contribution to the field of psychoanalysis

    **B**  his diverse output of artistic works

    **C**  his inappropriate behaviour and eccentricity

    **D**  his striking and unusual paintings

    **E**  his attempt to create popular accessible works

## Questions 19–21

*Choose the correct letter, A, B, C or D.*

19  What does the writer convey about Dali's childhood and student days?

   A   his inability to pursue a goal until its conclusion

   B   his mental instability, evident in his great ambition

   C   his supreme confidence in his own abilities

   D   his obviously superior intelligence

20  Why did critics turn against Dali?

   A   He had an obsession with fashionable clothing.

   B   He was devoting more time to TV commercials than painting.

   C   His work no longer did justice to his talent.

   D   His obsession with Surrealism overshadowed his work.

21  What does the writer convey about his own attitude towards Dali's life and work?

   A   He believes that, despite promising beginnings, Dali wasted his talents.

   B   In his opinion, few artists are interested in Dali's work.

   C   He thinks that people focused more on Dali's exhibitionist behaviour than his talent.

   D   He believes that despite his failings, Dali has left an enduring legacy.

## Questions 22–26

*Complete the summary below.*

*Use **NO MORE THAN TWO WORDS** from the passage for each answer.*

Dali has managed to achieve **22** .........................................., becoming the figurehead of the Surrealist Movement. His sheer **23** .........................................., which for some might have been interpreted as arrogance, led him to believe he was capable of achieving anything. Moving to France, where he encountered Surrealist artists, was a **24** ........................................... in his life. Dali's work was chiefly inspired by Freud's **25** ........................................... theories. However, as Dali became increasingly infatuated with money, the standard of his art declined. Despite the fact that his work is of varying quality, Dali will never **26** ........................................... .

## SECTION 3   Questions 27–40

*Read the text below and answer Questions 27–40.*

# Driverless cars

Driverless cars may be set to become a reality. At least, that is, if the executives behind the taxi app, Uber, are to be believed. Currently, Uber is taking its biggest steps yet towards a driver-free world, launching the Uber Advanced Technologies Centre in Pittsburgh. The ultimate goal of this institution is to 'do research and development, primarily in the areas of mapping and vehicle safety and autonomy technology'.

To date, Uber has provided a chauffeur-driven taxi service for their clients. Venturing into the realm of driverless cars is therefore a new direction which will require massive investment. It is indeed a huge leap of faith on Uber's part, since technology has yet to catch up with the idea of a fully autonomous vehicle. On the plus side, cars equipped with self-driving technology can already perform challenging manoeuvres like parking, as well as stay in lane and maintain a steady cruising speed. In a patchwork fashion, such cars could eventually build up to almost full automation, and Uber believes that car drivers will readily embrace the idea of driverless taxis. In Uber's eyes, current car owners only stand to gain by the introduction of such technology. Hiring a driverless cab means that the client does not have to pay for the cost of the driver in the cab fee. The only cost incurred by clients is for fuel, plus wear and tear. It is certainly an attractive proposition. Uber stands to benefit, too, since employees currently working as taxi drivers will be removed from the company's payroll. Apparently, for car drivers and Uber, it is a win-win situation.

Not everyone will benefit, however, from this technology, the car industry being an obvious example. Not surprisingly, the industry views the concept of self-driving cars with a sense of growing alarm. Such technology could well prove the death knell for private car ownership. As a result, the industry is dragging its feet over the manufacture and introduction of fully automated vehicles onto the market, due to commercial issues.

The commercial aspect apart, there is also the safety issue. Whilst a fully automated car could respond to most eventualities in the course of a trip, would it be capable of responding to unforeseen events, such as changes in route or unexpected diversions? Evidently, legislative authorities are also of this opinion.

Currently, no matter how much automation a car has, it still requires a driver with a full licence behind the wheel to drive on public roads. Whilst robot drivers, on the whole, have the upper hand on their human counterparts safety-wise, that still does not guarantee that they will become legal. As a consortium of researchers put it, 'If self-driving cars cut the roughly 40,000 annual US traffic fatalities in half, the carmakers might get not 20,000 thank-you notes, but 20,000 lawsuits'.

Interestingly, Uber are now undertaking an aggressive hiring campaign for taxi drivers to meet the demand for their taxi app. It seems that even Uber is less than confident that driverless taxis will soon become a reality. Whether Uber is backing a doomed campaign or instead is about to bring in a technology that will be universally greeted with positivity and acceptance depends entirely on your viewpoint.

John Reynolds, a Pittsburgh taxi driver, is angry at Uber's attitude on fully automated technology. 'They are completely disregarding individual livelihoods such as mine, as well as those of big car manufacturers, in the pursuit of money. Admittedly, things change and we have to roll with the times, but there should be some safeguards in place to protect those potentially affected by the introduction of new technologies. I guess I'm biased, being a taxi driver myself, but it's difficult to see it objectively.'

Susie Greenacre, a resident of Pittsburgh, has no such reservations about driverless cars. 'I'm all for it. Driverless cars have my backing any day! I hate the stress of rush-hour traffic! I think if I could just hop in a driverless car which would take me anywhere I wanted, I would never want to drive again!'

Jason Steiner, a school teacher in a secondary school, is inclined to agree with Susie. 'Whilst I'm not averse to driving, I would swap the stressful daily commute by car to a driverless one if I had the chance! It just takes the pressure off driving. I would be slightly wary, though, of being completely dependent on a robot-driven car when it comes to having to react to unexpected obstacles in the road'.

## Questions 27–32

*Choose the correct letter, A, B, C or D.*

27  Which of the following statements is accurate?

    A  Driverless cars conform to safety regulations.

    B  There is an obvious market for fully automated cars.

    C  Human drivers are no competition for driverless cars.

    D  Potentially, fully automated taxis are more cost-effective than normal taxis.

28  Uber is investing in a technology that

    A  will prove controversial.

    B  has been tried and tested.

    C  is unlikely to prove cost-effective.

    D  will be universally welcomed.

29  What is not true about driverless cars?

    A  They have become a reality in many countries.

    B  They may improve road safety.

    C  They will reduce the cost of travelling.

    D  They will endanger jobs.

30  What can be said about current legislation?

    A  It is in favour of driverless cars.

    B  It currently doesn't favour fully automated cars.

    C  It is keeping up with technology.

    D  It already accommodates driverless cars.

31  What is the general view held by car manufacturers?

    A  Driverless cars are more dangerous than non-automated cars.

    B  Fully automated cars are too expensive to manufacture.

    C  The introduction of driverless cars will threaten their livelihoods.

    D  Technology is still too underdeveloped to manufacture driverless cars.

32  What can be said about the writer's opinion of driverless cars?

    A  He is not really interested, but sceptical, that such a technology will be developed.

    B  He reserves judgement as to whether fully automated cars will become a reality.

    C  He believes that such a technology will never become a reality.

    D  He is critical of Uber's plans to introduce fully automated cars.

## Questions 33–37

*Look at the following statements 33–37 and the list of people below. Match each statement to the correct person, A–C. You may use any letter more than once.*

> A  John Reynolds
>
> B  Susie Greenacre
>
> C  Jason Steiner

33  This person can see the benefits of fully automated cars but has one particular concern.                    ................

34  This person would have no regrets about giving up driving entirely in favour of being driven by a fully automated car.                    ................

35  This person is aware that the new technology of driverless cars may not provide an adequate substitute for a human driver.                    ................

36  This person believes that those affected adversely by new technology should be protected from its effects.                    ................

37  This person enjoys driving but only under favourable conditions.                    ................

## Questions 38–40

*Do the following statements agree with the information given in the text? For questions 38–40, write*

> TRUE if the statement agrees with the information
>
> FALSE if the statement contradicts the information
>
> NOT GIVEN if there is no information on this

38  Driverless technology will have to overcome legal and safety obstacles to become completely viable.                    ................

39  Uber has shown nothing but complete self-conviction in its investment in driverless cars.                    ................

40  The safety issues with driverless technology are likely to be resolved fairly quickly.                    ................

# Writing

## WRITING TASK 1

*You should spend about 20 minutes on this task.*

The bar chart below gives information about the amount of tax that various arts and cultural organisations were required to pay last year.

> Summarise the information by selecting and reporting the main features and make comparisons where relevant.
>
> *Write at least 150 words.*

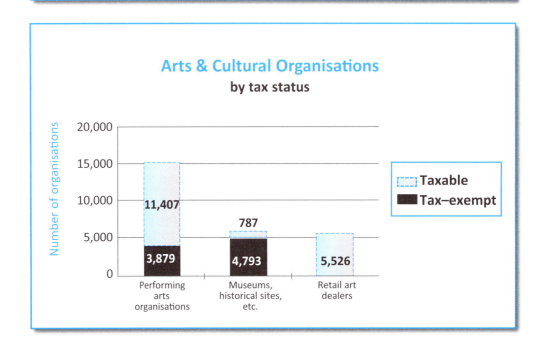

## WRITING TASK 2

*You should spend about 40 minutes on this task.*

*Write about the following topic:*

> Few artists ever manage to achieve fame, let alone a liveable wage.
> Often, artists struggle to make ends meet for most of their lives.
> For this reason, some people believe that it is irresponsible for a parent to encourage their child to pursue an artistic career. To what extent do you agree with this view?

*Give reasons for your answer and include any relevant examples from your own knowledge or experience.*

*Write at least 250 words.*

# Speaking

## PART 1 *(4–5 minutes)*

The examiner will ask you some questions about yourself, your home, work or studies and other familiar topics, for example:

- *Do you like art? Why/Why not?*
- *Do you have any artistic pursuits?*
- *Is it important for you to have a creative outlet? Why/Why not?*
- *Describe something that you made and are proud of.*
- *What would inspire you to be more creative?*

The examiner will then ask you some questions about other topics, for example:

### Now let's talk about your art education at school.

- *In your opinion, did you have good art teachers?*
- *Did you enjoy art lessons? Why/Why not?*
- *Was there enough time on the school curriculum for art lessons?*
- *Do you think more time should be spent on teaching art in school?*
- *Is there any art form not taught that you think has a place in the school curriculum?*
  *e.g., installation art/home movie-making*

## PART 2 *(2 minutes)*

The examiner will give you a topic on a card like the one shown here and ask you to talk about it for one to two minutes. Before you talk, you will have one minute to think about what you are going to say. The examiner will give you some paper and a pencil so you can make notes if you want to.

> Describe an artist who has impressed you in some way.
> You should say:
> - who the artist is
> - why he/she impressed you so much
> - what you like most about his/her work

The examiner may ask you one or two more questions when you have finished, for example:

- *Do you think this artist has had an effect on the way you view art?*
- *If you were an artist, would you try to produce the same type of art? Why/Why not?*

## PART 3 *(4–5 minutes)*

The examiner will then ask some more general questions which follow on from the topic in Part 2, for example:

- *Do you think it is easier to be an artist today than it was in the past?*
- *What problems do you think professional artists experience?*
- *Are artists given sufficient support by the public?*
- *In your opinion, were there more talented artists in the past?*
- *Do you think that artists are more interested in their art than in making money?*
- *Is it easy to become a celebrity artist nowadays?*
- *Do you think some celebrated artists today are overpaid?*
- *Do you believe that prestigious art prizes, like the Turner Prize, are given to deserving artists?*

# TEST 1

Narrator: You will hear a number of different recordings and you will have to answer questions based on what you hear. There will be time for you to read the instructions and questions and you will have a chance to check your work.
All the recordings will be played ONCE only. The test is in four sections. At the end of the test you will be given 10 minutes to transfer your answers to the Answer Sheet.
Now turn to Section 1.

## Section 1
You will hear a telephone conversation between a caller and a representative of a company hiring marquees. First you have some time to look at questions 1–7. [Pause – 30 seconds]
You will see that there is an example that has been done for you. On this occasion only, the conversation relating to this will be played first.

Representative: Good afternoon! Magnificent Marquees, how can I help you?
Caller: Oh, hello, I would like to hire a marquee. You see, it's for a special occasion. My eldest daughter is celebrating her 18th birthday and her coming of age. There was no question of her waiting until her 21st, although I'm sure we'll be having a big celebration then, too!
Representative: So, you're celebrating in style! Well, of course, I'd be happy to help. First, could you give me some details about guest numbers?

Narrator: The customer wants to hire a marquee for her eldest daughter's 18th birthday, so you write 'eldest daughter' in the space provided. You should answer the questions as you listen because you will not hear the recording a second time. Listen carefully and answer questions 1–7.

Representative: Good afternoon! Magnificent Marquees, how can I help you?
Caller: Oh, hello, I would like to hire a marquee. You see, it's for a special occasion. My eldest daughter is celebrating her 18th birthday and her coming of age. There was no question of her waiting until her 21st, although I'm sure we'll be having a big celebration then, too!
Representative: So, you're celebrating in style! Well, of course, I'd be happy to help. First, could you give me some details about guest numbers?
Caller: Right, yes ... Well, I was anticipating just a small 'do', but my daughter seems to have other ideas!
Representative: Well, you can't blame her; it's a special day!
Caller: I guess ... I told her to limit numbers to around 50 guests, but the guest list seems to be growing daily. She would like to invite double that number, but we decided to split the difference and settle on 80 (1) rather than 100!
Representative: If you don't mind some of the guests standing, then our marquee sizes always allow standing space for almost double as many as those seated. For instance, one of our smaller marquees seats 30 guests but accommodates 50 standing.
Caller: That sounds interesting. How big is that marquee? As not only am I working to a budget, but also we're limited by our garden size.
Representative: Can you give me an idea of both your budget and the size we're looking at?
Caller: Yes, I'm thinking of spending between £400 and £600. I can stretch to another hundred or two but that's the maximum limit (2). As for size, well, our garden is 15 metres by 30 metres.
Representative: OK ... Well, our 4.5 (3) by 9 metres marquee would fit in nicely. The hire and installation (4) comes to £450, but that allows you to have the marquee for two days.
Caller: The marquee size you mentioned sounds fine and will accommodate the guests that we are expecting. Yes, I think that's the size I'll go for.
Representative: So, now as to the cost of lighting and fittings ...
Caller: Oh, will that be very expensive?
Representative: It depends on what you want, but the cost of carpeting (5) the marquee will add on another £150. With regard to the lighting, prices vary quite a bit. If you opt for chandelier lighting, then it's another £90. But that's the most expensive option. Otherwise, the average pricing is around £55 (6).
Caller: I think I'll go for the more economic lighting then.
Representative: Then there's the furniture: tables and chairs and so on. You decided on seating for 30 guests ... Well, at £3 per chair, that will work out at £90 in total. You will then probably need five tables at least and so with each table costing £4, that brings us to a total of £20 for the tables.
Caller: OK, so I'm still just within my budget. Great! I'll go ahead with the booking then.
Representative: Wonderful. So there's only one more important detail that I need. When would you like us to set up the marquee?
Caller: Well, my daughter's birthday is on June 6th, so ideally a day beforehand. (7) Then we could have it taken down the day after her birthday.
Representative: Yes, no problem.
Caller: Great. Well, I'll go ahead with the order then.
Representative: Wonderful!

Narrator: Before listening to the rest of the conversation, you have some time to look at questions 8–10. [Pause – 30 seconds]
Now listen and answer questions 8–10.

Representative: OK, so that I can process your order, I need to take down some details. May I start by taking down your name and postcode?
Caller: Yes. It's Jenny Lakewell (8), and the postcode's CV6 TL3 (9).
Representative: Is that Jenny with a double n?
Caller: Yes, that's correct.
Representative: And is that Jenny with a y or an ie at the end?
Caller: Yes, it confuses everyone. I use the first spelling.
Representative: And, I'm sorry. I didn't quite catch the postcode, was that 'CB6?'
Caller: No, it's with a V, not a B. So it's CV6.
Representative: Right you are. Can I have a contact number also, please?
Caller: My mobile number is 0-7-9-0-0 4-5-6. Oh, hold on a minute! I forgot I've got a different number now. So it's 0-7-9- then double 4, not double 0, followed by 3-2-5-8-8-3. (10)
Representative: Great! That's everything for the moment. We will be sending you details and an invoice through the post in the next few days.
Caller: OK. And thank you for your help. Goodbye!

Narrator: That's the end of Section 1. You have half a minute to check your answers. [Pause – 30 seconds]
Now turn to Section 2.

## Section 2
You will hear a history teacher talking to students in a class. First you will have time to look at questions 11–15.
[Pause – 30 seconds]
Now listen carefully and answer questions 11–15.

Today we are going to study the typical layout of a medieval English castle. Highly fortified and with difficult access, medieval castles were impressive strongholds, designed to keep the castle's inhabitants safe and the invaders at bay.
The main entrance would have been the Outer Gatehouse, located at the bottom right-hand corner of the diagram just by the chapel buildings. (11) However, even if you had entered via the Outer Gatehouse into the castle grounds, you would still have been outside the main part of the castle. The buildings in the Outer Court were not the main residential areas of the castle. These latter buildings belonged to the inner castle area and were heavily protected both by a water-filled channel known as a 'moat', which extended around a third of the inner part of the castle, as well as the fortified walls around the castle exterior.
To enter the innermost area you had to enter a long, narrow tunnel known as a barbican, over, and directly above

which, the Gatehouse was located. The barbican, being the only access point to the inner castle, was narrow and heavily guarded to prevent large enemy forces storming the inner castle area. The inner castle area held the main buildings around which daily life revolved. Here, the Great Hall, along with the Great Chambers and Kitchens, were located, as well as the castle Bakehouse. (11,12,13) The Great Hall was a building with a courtyard view to the back and front. (12) Whilst the Great Hall enjoyed a central location in the inner castle area, the Great Chambers and Kitchen were less prominently positioned (13). Both of the latter buildings were located off to either side of the Great Hall. The Great Chambers, unlike the Bakehouse, which is next to one of the towers, did not enjoy a courtyard view. (13,14) Part of the exterior castle wall formed the back wall of the Great Chambers, as it did with the Stables, located in the Outer Court. (15)

Narrator: **Before you hear the rest of the discussion you have some time to look at questions 16–20. [Pause – 30 seconds] Now listen and answer questions 16–20.**

The layout I have just described will give you a better idea as to the design of a medieval castle. There was no blueprint for castles though, and the design and layout of each castle was determined greatly by local demands, function and purpose for which the fortification was intended. (16) What we see in the castle design here is an advance on earlier medieval designs. Those medieval castles that predated this one had very basic residential and living areas. In such castles, the main focal point was the Keep rather than the Great Hall and Great Chambers, as in later years. Little more than a fortified tower, the Keep doubled up as basic accommodation for the castle's residents. (17) As the years passed, the living areas became more luxurious, evolving into separate buildings. (18)

Confusingly, the Keep was known as a 'donjon', meaning fortified tower, in French. The term 'dungeon' was only used in later years to refer to underground prisons. In fact, at the time when the Keep dominated castle affairs, the use of latter-day dungeons for imprisonment was an unknown and alien concept (19), the judicial systems favouring more physical forms of punishment instead.

Another dissimilarity between earlier and later medieval castles was in their fortification. A moat, fortified walls and a barbican were typical features of most castles. However, it was recognised with the passage of time that the narrow, fortified entrance of the barbican was insufficient defence against an enemy intent on invading the castle (20). As a result, extra, more reliable fortifications were added in the form of a portcullis and a drawbridge. The portcullis was a spiked metal gate that could be dropped vertically down from under the gatehouse, thereby sealing off the inner castle entrance from the outside world. To protect the main castle entrance further, a drawbridge was placed in front of the portcullis. This was a retractable bridge between the gatehouse and the outside area of the castle. However, the portcullis always remained the last line of defence against the enemy.

Narrator: **That's the end of Section 2. You have half a minute to check your answers. [Pause – 30 seconds] Now turn to Section 3.**

## Section 3
**You will hear a discussion between two literature students and their lecturer. First you have some time to look at questions 21–25. [Pause – 30 seconds] Now listen carefully and answer questions 21–25.**

**Julie:** That was an interesting lecture.
**Lecturer:** I'm glad you thought so.
**Dave:** Yes, it made a break from the usual lectures on literary style. It certainly made me look at some of Shakespeare's plays, like *Hamlet*, and the playwright himself in a new light. (21)
**Julie:** Me too! I always thought that Shakespeare believed in the supernatural and that was the reason why so many of his plays, like *Hamlet* and *Macbeth*, featured a ghost.
**L:** What you thought is a common misconception. However,

when you think about it, it was unlikely that Shakespeare would have been sympathetic to a belief in ghosts.
**Dave:** Why?
**L:** Well, he was Protestant, as was his audience, and the Protestant religion did not subscribe to a belief in ghosts as spirits returning from another world. Also, *Hamlet* was set in Denmark and, although fictional, the play would have reflected the Protestant beliefs of the Danes, too. (22)
**Julie:** So, the main religion in England at the time was Protestantism?
**L:** Very much so. Any other religions, like Catholicism, were not tolerated by the religious authorities or James I, who was head of the Church of England at the time. (23)
**Julie:** What did the Catholics believe about ghosts?
**L:** Their religion was compatible with a belief in the spirit world, as it were. Ghosts were seen as lost souls that were in Purgatory; that is to say, a state between Heaven and Hell.
**Julie:** So it was obvious, really, that Shakespeare incorporated ghosts into his play for other reasons, right?
**L:** Absolutely. It's certainly odd to write about something you really don't believe in and then ask the audience to believe in it. So, yes, there was clearly another motive.
**Julie:** I guess when you think about it, it's quite apparent. As you mentioned in the lecture, ghosts appear in *Macbeth* and *Hamlet* really to show what the characters are thinking and as a catalyst for certain events. (24)
**L:** Quite right.
**Dave:** And I think it's quite plain that Shakespeare had no belief in the supernatural. The fact that the ghosts seen by Macbeth and Hamlet are only often either visible to themselves or speak only to them suggests that the ghosts are only as real as the imagination of those who see them.
**Julie:** So would you say that the audience was as sceptical as Shakespeare with regard to ghosts?
**L:** Well, as you know, the official line would have been that they didn't believe in ghosts, as it was not in line with Protestant beliefs prevalent at the time. Nevertheless, contrary to expectations, they do seem to have been a superstitious lot. (25) Belief in witches and astrology were common back then, but how they justified their beliefs in religious terms is quite a mystery.

Narrator: **Before you hear the rest of the discussion you have some time to look at questions 26–30. [Pause – 30 seconds] Now listen and answer questions 26–30.**

**Julie:** People, I think, today are a lot less gullible than in that period though, don't you agree? I mean, honestly! Believing in witches and astrology and all that … (26)
**L:** Well, judging by the popularity of TV programmes today like 'Most Haunted', I would say there's a fair amount of interest in the supernatural still.
**Julie:** I guess most people are like me – curious, but not entirely convinced when it comes to the spirit world. (27)
**Dave:** Well, I think ghosts are just the product of certain people's imaginations!
**Julie:** You can't overlook the fact that many supernatural events cannot be explained.
**Dave:** Personally, I think ghosts are just as likely to exist as UFOs and aliens.
**L:** Well, I think at least the latter do exist.
**Julie:** I agree, it's absurd to think we are alone in the universe. (28)
**Dave:** Hmmm …
**L:** You certainly seem to be quite a sceptic, Dave.
**Dave:** Actually, I do believe in some aspects of the paranormal …
**Julie:** Like?
**Dave:** Well, not ghosts and aliens, obviously, but things like telepathy and premonition.
**Julie:** It's easier to understand or believe in telepathy and premonition as you hear of so many examples of these phenomena occurring in real life. Not just reported stories but from friends and acquaintances. I'm inclined, though, to think premonitions are more coincidence than due to a paranormal event. But maybe I'm just saying that, as I've not had first-hand experience of premonitions. (29)

## Audio Script

**Dave:** <u>So, you believe in telepathy then?</u>
**Julie:** <u>I think that the evidence in favour of it is impossible to deny.</u> (30) What do you think, Miss?
**L:** Maybe I'm less sceptical than most, but I'm inclined to keep a pretty open mind on most things. Anyway, it's been a very interesting discussion, but I'm afraid I have to leave now as I'm due to give another lecture.
**Julie:** Well, thank you for your time, and also your wonderful lecture!
**Dave:** Yes, thank you, we appreciated it!
**L:** My pleasure!

**Narrator:** That's the end of Section 3. You have half a minute to check your answers. *[Pause – 30 seconds]*
Now turn to Section 4.

## Section 4
You will hear part of a lecture about Darwin's theory of evolution and its impact on society. First you have some time to look at questions 31–40. *[Pause – 1 minute]*
Now listen carefully and answer questions 31–40.

Today, few people can be unaware of Darwin and his theory of evolution. He single-handedly revolutionised the way we think about the <u>natural world</u>. (31)

However, when I say 'single-handedly', that is not entirely correct. At precisely the same time as Darwin was formulating his theory of evolution, another scientist, Alfred Russell Wallace, was working on a virtually <u>identical theory</u> (32) in parallel to Darwin. However, whilst Darwin's name has been preserved for posterity, the name of Wallace is virtually unknown. Why one should have been celebrated in scientific circles whilst the other was relegated to obscurity is puzzling. Both decided to make their discoveries public in a joint announcement once they were made aware of one another's work. There is no question that Darwin acted dishonourably, therefore, falsely claiming the <u>sole credit</u> (33) for a theory of evolution. However, the publication of Darwin's ground-breaking 'On the Origin of Species by Natural Selection' the following year almost certainly helped to secure him enduring fame.

The publication of Darwin's book proved to be a watershed in the history of science. It also proved extremely <u>controversial</u> (34) in the eyes of the Church since Darwin claimed that Man was merely an animal, *homo sapiens,* and a product <u>of evolution</u> (35) rather than of divine intervention. Such a theory was in direct opposition to religious dogmas of the day and threatened to undermine the very core of religious belief.

Today, however, many have successfully managed to reconcile Darwin's theory of evolution with religion. Only for some people, known as 'Creationists', is Darwin's theory seen as being incompatible with religion. For these individuals, Darwin's theory is seen as heretical since they believe in a literal interpretation of the Bible and a biblical reference to the world being created in seven days rather than as a slow evolutionary process spanning millions of years. In addition, Darwin's claim that Man is no more than a highly evolved ape is regarded as a blasphemy, since Creationists insist on the divine origin of Man.

Whilst not many would dispute Darwin's theory of evolution nowadays, curiously, an ape-man that bridges the gap between Man and ape has yet to be found. The search for the <u>'missing link'</u> (36), as it has been called, has both occupied and perplexed scientists since the time of Darwin. Many hoaxers over the years have tried to exploit the desire of scientists to find conclusive <u>proof of</u> (37) Darwin's theory in the form of a missing link. The most memorable and also convincing hoax was that of the Piltdown Man. Named after the Sussex village where it was first unearthed in 1908, the skull of the Piltdown Man represented a transition from an ape to a man. <u>So convincing</u> (38) a hoax was it that it fooled the scientific establishment into believing for some 40 years that the 'missing link' had indeed been found. In fact, the

*Manchester Guardian* newspaper went so far as to call the discovery of the ape-man skull 'by far the earliest trace of mankind that has yet been found in England'.

The find was credited to a local solicitor and fossil hunter, Charles Dawson. When Dawson died in 1916, Piltdown Man's place in history seemed secure. In 1950, a reconstruction of a head was made based on the skull. However, only three years later, the skull was declared <u>a fake</u> (39). People later questioned how such a hoax could have escaped detection without the compliance of an expert.

It is certainly an interesting footnote in the theory of evolution. However, the questions <u>still remain</u> (40) today: where is the missing link and why hasn't it been found?

**Narrator:** That is the end of Section 4. You now have half a minute to check your answers. *[Pause – 30 seconds]*
That is the end of the listening test. You now have 10 minutes to transfer your answers to the Listening Answer Sheet.

# TEST 2

**Narrator:** You will hear a number of different recordings and you will have to answer questions based on what you hear. There will be time for you to read the instructions and questions and you will have a chance to check your work.
All the recordings will be played ONCE only. The test is in four sections. At the end of the test you will be given 10 minutes to transfer your answers to the Answer Sheet.
Now turn to Section 1.

## Section 1
You will hear a woman talking to a man who works in a tourist information office. First you have some time to look at questions 1–10. *[Pause – 30 seconds]*
You will see that there is an example that has been done for you. On this occasion only, the conversation relating to this will be played first.

*Man: Good afternoon. Can I help you?*
*Woman: I hope so! My Portuguese friends are coming over to visit me next month and I need to find a place for them to stay that is quite central as I live in the city centre myself and want them to be close by. Can you recommend anywhere?*
*Man: Yes. A few places instantly spring to mind. What about Belvedere Gardens Hotel? Despite what the name might suggest, it's right in the city centre, on Main Street, opposite Grimes Tower.*

**Narrator:** The Belvedere Gardens Hotel is located opposite Grimes Tower, so you write *opposite* in the space provided. You should answer the questions as you listen because you will not hear the recording a second time. Listen carefully and answer questions 1–6.

**Man:** Good afternoon. Can I help you?
**Woman:** I hope so! My Portuguese friends are coming over to visit me next month and I need to find a place for them to stay that is quite central as I live in the city centre myself and want them to be close by. Can you recommend anywhere?
**Man:** Yes. A few places instantly spring to mind. What about Belvedere Gardens Hotel? Despite what the name might suggest, it's right in the city centre; on Main Street, opposite Grimes Tower.
**Woman:** How much is it per night, please?
**Man:** Quite reasonable given the location; $50, and that is inclusive of a <u>continental</u> (1) breakfast.
**Woman:** Oh, that sounds nice! What about other meals? Do you have to pay extra for them?
**Man:** Yes. Unfortunately, lunch and dinner are not included in the price. The hotel does have a very fine restaurant, though, and I would thoroughly recommend the <u>buffet dinner</u> (2) there; customers should be seated by 7:30 in the evening when the buffet starts.
**Woman:** Hmm. I'll keep it in mind. Is there anywhere else you can think of?
**Man:** Certainly. The Belfield Grande is always a popular

choice. It's located a little further out, though; on the south side of Edgeware Common (3). Perhaps that's too far from the city centre.

**Woman:** Not really; it's only a few stops on the subway; depends on the price.

**Man:** Believe it or not, the Belfield is more expensive than the Belvedere Gardens, $55.

**Woman:** Oh, that's no good.

**Man:** Mind you, there is a $10 discount offered to customers who have booked online (4). There's also the fact that the price is inclusive of all meals (5) (breakfast, lunch and dinner) served in the guests' lounge (6).

**Narrator: Before listening to the rest of the conversation you have some time to look at questions 7–10. [Pause – 30 seconds]
Now listen and answer questions 7–10.**

**Woman:** I like the sound of this hotel more and more. The Belfield then, so far. Is there anywhere else?

**Man:** Well, you should also consider the Maple View (7).

**Woman:** I don't think I am familiar with that one.

**Man:** You should be; it's right in the heart of the city, next to the entrance to the pedestrian (8) zone that runs along High Street.

**Woman:** Sounds lovely, being so close to the shops. Tell me more.

**Man:** It gets better; the price per night is only $28 on weekdays, though an additional $12 is charged on weekends and bank holidays (9).

**Woman:** Sounds like great value for money.

**Man:** It is; that's why you have to book well in advance (10) of your stay.

**Woman:** How soon should I book then?

**Man:** Yesterday might not be soon enough!

**Woman:** Yikes! I better get cracking. Thank you so much for your help.

**Man:** You're very welcome.

**Narrator: That's the end of Section 1. You have half a minute to check your answers. [Pause – 30 seconds]
Now turn to Section 2.**

## Section 2
**You will hear a tour leader talking to some tourists. First you will have some time to look at questions 11–16. [Pause – 30 seconds]
Now listen carefully and answer questions 11–16.**

OK, ladies and gentlemen, may I have your attention, please? So here we are at King's Cross Station. We'll be leaving from here in just over an hour to catch a tube from the Underground station, so you'll have a bit of time to look around.

But first things first. Just so as you can get your bearings and find your way around this rather complex and confusing Station, I will point out essential areas as well as points of interest.

At the moment, we are standing in King's Cross Square, facing two main exit doors, one off to our left and the other off to our right. The exits lead from the main platform area which can be accessed by several entrances, one of which is located just a bit further away, to your left, although it is obscured by a wall from where we're standing. Oh, by the way, that building standing on its own (the larger, not the smaller one) on your far left is the Great Northern Hotel. The taxi rank is sandwiched between it and the Left Luggage Office. (11) So, before I go onto a description of the main shopping and platform areas on the other side of the station wall, I'd like to point out the most important point of all: the Underground Station (12), which is where we need to meet promptly for departure. Luckily, it's quite prominent as it's located away from the shopping and platform area of the station. It's just over there on the corner, in between the entrance I mentioned earlier and the exit nearest to the hotel from where we're standing now. (12)

Now for those of you who would like to grab a bite to eat or do a bit of shopping, you can enter the shopping area by that entrance door over there. It's by far the nearest entrance. You will find several clothes shops in this area in addition to a fast food outlet. When you go in the entrance, if you go straight ahead rather than turning left into the other part of the shopping complex, you will find two buildings facing one another. Within these buildings are several shops and eating places. In the building immediately after the ticket barriers on your right you will find that the first shop you come across is the fast food outlet, Burgerland. (13) If you need to avail yourself of the toilet facilities, then carry straight on past Burgerland and they're at the far end of the building. In between the toilets and the ticket office is the Disabled Meeting Point. (14) You will have to enter through this area in order to gain access to the toilets.

If you would like to go up to the second floor, where there are one or two shops and a pizzeria, then as you enter the shopping area through the main entrance, instead of going straight ahead, you turn off to the left. The escalators are immediately on your left again. When you go up the escalators, you will see two buildings again on your left. Go past the first building and the pizzeria is the first shop that you come to, in the second building. (15)

Now, I would just like to ask; are there any Harry Potter fans with us today? Ah, good. Yes, I see several hands raised. Well, there's a treat in store for you if you go to the far end of the second building and take the escalator down again to the ground floor. As you reach the bottom of the escalator, turn right and carry on walking, keeping the ticket barrier on your left all the time. Don't turn off left but carry on walking until you find yourself up against the station wall. This is the famous Platform 9¾ (16) immortalised by J.K. Rowling in her Harry Potter books. You'll see half a trolley embedded in the wall to mark the spot.

So those are the main things to do and see. I hope you enjoy yourselves but please meet me at the Underground entrance promptly for departure. Don't be tempted to board the Hogwart Express on Platform 9¾!

**Narrator: Before you hear the rest of the discussion you have some time to look at questions 17–20. [Pause – 30 seconds]
Now listen and answer questions 17–20.**

Good, welcome back! I'm glad you were all punctual. As you know, we have a packed itinerary which will give you a 'taster' of London's major landmarks. (17)

Before we enter the Underground, I would just like to give you some important information. Firstly, for those of you unfamiliar with the London Underground, you must retain your ticket throughout the journey, (18) only surrendering the ticket at your final destination. This is not applicable to today's trip, but really for tomorrow when you will be at leisure and may wish to use the Underground again. For today, we have a group ticket which means that we have to stay together at all times whilst travelling on the Underground. Should you become separated from the group and end up travelling without a ticket, you can expect to pay a hefty fine.

Also, remember that while we are travelling outside the rush hour, between 5 and 7 p.m. in the evening and from 7.30 and 9 a.m. in the morning, (19) we will still meet with the midday crowds of shoppers. Sometimes there is only standing room at such times, so you will be lucky to get a seat at all. Priority seats do exist if you are unable to stand, although this is rarely enforced and is at the discretion of the passenger occupying such seats. (20) Beware of pickpockets, too! There are many opportunist thieves who prey on unsuspecting travellers. Obviously, keep your valuables tucked away ensuring wallets, etc., are not visible.

So, that's all for now. Let's get on with the tour! Follow me and please keep close to your group members to avoid getting separated!

**Narrator: That's the end of Section 2. You have half a minute to check your answers. [Pause – 30 seconds]
Now turn to Section 3.**

| Audio Script |
| --- |

## Section 3

You will hear a discussion between Steve and Melisa about their commerce course. First you have some time to look at questions 21–25. *[Pause – 30 seconds]*
Now listen carefully and answer questions 21–25.

**Steve:** Hey Melisa! How's it going?
**Melisa:** Great; I'm really pleased to have the exams behind me; now I'm looking forward to a break for the summer as I know next year is going to be unbelievably difficult, being our final year and all. You?
**Steve:** Same – pleased to be finished, but dreading next year, though.
**Melisa:** Well, I wouldn't exactly say I'm dreading it, but I know what you're saying!
**Steve:** At least we're gonna have smaller classes next semester.
**Melisa:** How do you mean?
**Steve:** Didn't you hear? <u>The Commerce Faculty just got approval to build a new state-of-the-art lecture building over the summer months. It's expected to be finished by the start of term.</u> (21)
**Melisa:** Fantastic! No more lecture theatres crammed with over 200 people. That'll make a pleasant change. <u>How on earth are they paying for it, though? I thought the college was reining in its expenditure and decreasing spending.</u>
**Steve:** <u>It is, but the grant has been approved for the best part of three years,</u> (22,23) so they have no choice but to provide it now that the project is going ahead; after all, those funds are supposed to have been set aside especially.
**Melisa:** So what's taken so long for construction to start?
**Steve:** You see, the grant only covers 30% of the cost. The incoming government made a pledge during the election campaign that it would cover the other 70%, but, typical of a political party, wouldn't you know, it didn't keep its promise. The College Donors Club, a group of wealthy alumni, stepped in to pledge 10% of the money needed, <u>but the project really only got a kick-start when an anonymous donor pledged the rest.</u> (22,23)
**Melisa:** Very mysterious!
**Steve:** Yeah, and apparently he demanded that certain changes be made to the plans before handing over the money.
**Melisa:** Like what?
**Steve:** <u>Well, you know the proposal to have a gym in the basement?</u>
**Melisa:** <u>Don't tell me that's been cancelled.</u>
**Steve:** <u>Not at all. In fact, our anonymous donor friend insisted on it being twice the original size and on a relaxation room being added as well.</u> (24,25) You know, with games and stuff.
**Melisa:** Sweet! Are we still getting our new computer lab? There's always such an awful queue for the existing one.
**Steve:** We are indeed and next to it there's now going to be what they're calling the Software Zone. A place where students can access all the latest high-end software free of charge.
**Melisa:** Nice! Thank you very much, Mr. Donor! Everything else is staying, right? Lecture rooms, hardware zone, etc.?
**Steve:** Yeah. The rest's the same.

**Narrator:** Before you hear the rest of the discussion you have some time to look at questions 26–30. *[Pause – 30 seconds]*
Now listen and answer questions 26–30.

**Melisa:** By the way, on the subject of college next year, Steve, have you decided what courses you are going to choose yet?
**Steve:** Pretty much. I want to major in marketing, so <u>I'm focusing on the International Markets and Product Placement modules</u> (26,27). Will you be joining me?
**Melisa:** Well, you know I prefer Human Resources; that'll probably be my major, but if you twist my arm, <u>I'll probably join you for the first one</u> (26); <u>no way on all that Product Placement nonsense, though</u> (27), sounds boring! <u>Organisational Behaviour is a requirement if you want to major in HR, as is Managing People, so I will definitely do both of those.</u> (28,29) Will you join me on them then?

**Steve:** Sorry, Melisa; you know HR is just not my thing. What about your optional modules? Do you feel like doing Information Systems with me? We all need to know a bit about the digital world, after all!
**Melisa:** Hmm. <u>I'll get back to you! I haven't ruled out Public Relations, either</u> (30). Let's chat about it again later in the week when I've had some time to think.
**Steve:** Cool; I'll call you, OK?
**Melisa:** Sounds like a plan! I'd better go now.

**Narrator:** That's the end of Section 3. You have half a minute to check your answers. *[Pause – 30 seconds]*
Now turn to Section 4.

## Section 4

You will hear part of a talk on some well–known personality tests and their uses. First you have some time to look at questions 31–40. *[Pause – 1 minute]*
Now listen carefully and answer questions 31–40.

I'm sure at some point in your lives you will have completed a personality test, whether for professional reasons or purely for fun. Such personality assessments are abundant. They pervade our <u>everyday lives</u> (31) since there is a fundamental human need to understand the motivation behind our own and others' behaviour. Learning how to assess personality permits greater understanding of the motivating factors affecting the way we communicate and <u>cooperate with</u> (32) others, in addition to how we relate to others on a personal level. So now that we've talked about why personality tests are so important, let's take a look at the most well-known tests and see how they compare.

Well, first-off we have a favourite of careers officers and potential employers alike – the Graphology Test. The word 'graphology' is derived from two Greek words meaning 'writing' and 'word'. Essentially, it is an assessment of personality based on <u>handwriting</u> (33) analysis. How an individual dots his i's or crosses his t's, in addition to whether writing is slanted or level, is believed to be indicative of the individual's personality. Whatever your opinion may be of this method of personality assessment, at least it has stood the test of time. The Graphology Test as a measure of personality was first proposed by a certain Juan Huartede San Juan as far back as 1575, and it has seen fluctuation in its popularity since then. In the 20th century, Alfred Binet was so convinced as to its validity that he termed it the 'science of the future', and indeed today, it is still a very popular method of personality assessment. Its validity though, as a measurement of character, is dubious. The British Psychological Society has even gone so far as to rank graphology alongside astrology, giving them both '<u>zero</u> validity' (34). A major problem with the test is that an element of subjectivity enters the assessment of certain criteria in the test, such as 'harmony' and 'style' of writing. However, in its favour, the test is relatively quick and easy to administer.

Next, let's look at the Rorschach or Ink Blot Test, which is one of the better known tools of psychological assessment. Popularised in party game versions of the test, the Rorschach Test has received mixed reactions amongst psychologists. Whilst many dismiss the test as a 'pseudoscience,' it is nevertheless used by prestigious <u>mental health</u> (35) organisations, such as the Tavistock Clinic, as a valid tool for personality assessment. Admittedly, assessing someone's character based on their reactions to a series of ink blots on pieces of card might seem somewhat ludicrous. Whilst there is a tried and tested methodology behind the construction of the test and assessment of individual responses, the test is subject to <u>cultural</u> (36) bias. The perception of the cards' contents are liable to be biased by cultural factors, making the individual responses somewhat meaningless.

So, moving onto a test that has similar features to the Rorschach Test, let's look at the Luscher Colour Test. As with the former test, the Luscher Colour Test assesses an individual's subjective reaction to a series of cards. However, unlike the Rorschach, the Luscher Test consists of a series of <u>coloured cards</u> (37) that the individual has to rank in order of preference. How the individual ranks the different colours is believed to be indicative of their personality. Whilst some believe the test to smack of pseudoscience and many question its validity, there is, however, a biological basis to the test which makes it more of a <u>convincing tool</u> (38) of psychological assessment than many other personality tests. Certainly, its use by psychologists and doctors, as well as authorities such as government agencies and universities to screen their candidates, would seem to be a strong argument for the validity of the test. A major plus to this test is that it is so accurate that it is even sensitive to mood change. Individuals, therefore, taking the same test at different periods of time will see a correlation between results and mood.

Finally, I would like to refer to the TAT, or the Thematic Apperception Test, to give it its full name. On the face of it, it is a very simplistic test. As with the Rorschach and Luscher tests, the individual is dealt a series of cards. However, on these cards are depicted a series of ambiguous scenes involving groups <u>of people</u> (39). The individual is required to make up a story about each, and the individual is then assessed based on the content of each story. Whilst the test is quick and simple to administer, critics of the test argue that there is a <u>lack</u> (40) of standardisation of the cards and scoring systems, making comparisons between individuals problematic. This, therefore, undermines the validity of the test. Nevertheless, the TAT is still used as a tool in fields as diverse as psychological research into occupation preference and partner selection and forensic examinations to evaluate crime suspects.

It is therefore a matter of individual preference as to which test is used when employed for professional reasons. All these tests, though, have their benefits and their drawbacks. No one definitive test exists that provides 100% accuracy in assessing personality.

**Narrator: That is the end of Section 4. You now have half a minute to check your answers. [Pause – 30 seconds]**
**That is the end of the listening test. You now have 10 minutes to transfer your answers to the Listening Answer Sheet.**

# TEST 3

**Narrator: You will hear a number of different recordings and you will have to answer questions based on what you hear. There will be time for you to read the instructions and questions, and you will have a chance to check your work.**
**All the recordings will be played ONCE only. The test is in four sections. At the end of the test you will be given 10 minutes to transfer your answers to the Answer Sheet.**
**Now turn to Section 1.**

## Section 1
You will hear part of a conversation between an art auctioneer and their client. First you have some time to look at questions 1–7. [Pause – 30 seconds]
You will see that there is an example that has been done for you. On this occasion only, the conversation relating to this will be played first.

*Auctioneer: Good afternoon, Madam. Ah yes, I see you successfully bid for Lot 2374.*
*Client: Good afternoon. Yes, that's correct.*

**Narrator: The Lot number of the auctioned article is 2374, so you write 2374 in the space provided. You should answer the questions as you listen because you will not hear the recording a second time. Listen carefully and answer questions 1–7.**

Auctioneer: Good afternoon, Madam. Ah yes, I see you successfully bid for Lot 2374.
Client: Good afternoon. Yes, that's correct.
Auctioneer: I hope you are satisfied with your purchase? If I may say so myself, I think you got a real bargain. What you

paid is not much above the original reserve price of <u>£300</u> (1)!
Client: I love P.J. <u>Browning's</u> (2) work and to be honest I was prepared to pay a lot more. <u>I'd decided beforehand that £500 would be my limit, so getting it £150 cheaper than I was prepared to pay for it was a wonderful surprise!</u> (3)
Auctioneer: I have to say that <u>17th-century</u> (4) paintings of rural <u>English</u> (5) scenes like this one are rather underrated. The art world seems to want abstract paintings by modern artists more. Geometric designs seem to be the trend today!
Client: Not my taste at all! I have a more conservative taste when it comes to art. The painting will blend in with my antique furniture at home.
Auctioneer: Well, I hope you have a big wall to put it on!
Client: Luckily, I'm very fortunate to live in a rather large country house. What are the exact measurements of the painting, by the way?
Auctioneer: The width is <u>1.5 metres</u> (6) and <u>the height is 1 metre, without the frame, that is. If you include the gilt-covered frame, which is quite large to balance the size of the painting, you can add on another 0.5 metres</u> (7) for the width and the same again for the height, obviously.
Client: That shouldn't prove too much of a problem. I'm just happy I managed to win the bid for this wonderful painting!

**Narrator: Before listening to the rest of the conversation you have some time to look at questions 8–10. [Pause – 30 seconds]**
**Now listen and answer questions 8–10.**

Auctioneer: So, madam, I would just like to take down some details from you.
Client: OK, go ahead!
Auctioneer: I recognise your face as you've attended several of our auctions before, but I can't put a name to your face. Could you remind me of your name, please?
Client: Oh, yes, it's Mrs <u>Bradwell–Thompson</u> (8). It's a double-barreled surname, so you need a hyphen in between the two surnames, you see.
Auctioneer: So that's spelt B-R-A-D-W-E-L-L followed by a hyphen, then T-H-O-M-S-O-N?
Client: Well the first part's right. But you spell Thompson with a P in between the M and the S of the surname.
Auctioneer: OK … and your address, please?
Client: Yes, it's Charlton Manor, that's spelt C-H-A-R-L-T-O-N, and I live in Kingston Village. Oh, and of course you'll need the postcode, too. It's <u>KN26 56T</u> (9).
Auctioneer: Sorry, did you say KM26 56T?
Client: No, it's K-N, not an M, then 2-6 5-6-T.
Auctioneer: Well, thank you, Mrs Bradwell–Thompson, I think that's just about everything. Oh, and I need to know when you would like the painting delivered. We deliver on Tuesdays and Fridays, the week following an auction.
Client: Well, I'm having a long weekend break in the Cotswolds, a charming area of England, you know, so this coming Friday would be impossible. How about next Tuesday?
Auctioneer: No problem at all, madam. So that will be <u>the 23rd of March</u> (10).
Client: Superb! Thank you.
Auctioneer: Not at all, madam. It was a pleasure doing business with you.

**Narrator: That's the end of Section 1. You have half a minute to check your answers. [Pause – 30 seconds]**
**Now turn to Section 2.**

## Section 2
You will hear the curator of an art museum talking to a group of visitors who are visiting the museum for the first time. First you will have time to look at questions 11–15.
[Pause – 30 seconds]
Now listen carefully and answer questions 11–15.

Curator: A very good afternoon to you all, ladies and gentlemen! I'm glad you've chosen to visit the prestigious Triton Museum of Art today, and I'll look forward to showing you around. But first, I would just like you to refer to the maps of the museum that you picked up on your way in.

## Audio Script

Now, where you picked up your maps is just to the left as you enter the building, outside the Museum Store. By the way, the store is a great place to pick up some souvenirs before you leave. Oh, and if anyone wants to leave a coat in the cloakroom, then please feel free to do so at no extra charge. It's just over there on the other side of the entrance to the Museum Store. (11)

OK. So this nice spacious area we're now standing in is the Rotunda. It contains some of the museum's most striking sculptures. From here, you gain access to all the museum. Leading off from the Rotunda are the Warburton Gallery and our other large gallery that houses a permanent art collection. We'll be starting our tour actually in the Permanent Collection Gallery as it's the nearest of the two galleries to the entrance. (12) We'll make our way afterwards to the other gallery I mentioned, as it's right next door. Oh, the smaller room behind the Warburton Gallery that you see on your maps is just a storage space for the museum and access is blocked off to the public by a railing across the entrance to that area. (13)

So now, where were we? Ah yes. After we've visited those galleries, which will take us a good hour as there are so many interesting exhibits to see, we'll make our way back across the Rotunda and visit the Cowell Room. It's right at the far end of the museum on the opposite side of the Rotunda to the Warburton and Permanent Collection galleries. (14) It's one of the museum highlights and contains some high-quality contemporary art exhibits. Oh, I'm so sorry, I forgot to point out the ladies and gents toilets earlier. They're just before you get to the Cowell Room and are adjacent to the Museum Store. Don't go into the room opposite the toilets. That's our staff room area and kitchen! (15) Right, so that's all you need to know for the moment. Let's begin the tour!

Narrator: Before you hear the rest of the discussion you have some time to look at questions 16–20. *[Pause – 30 seconds]*
Now listen and answer questions 16–20.

Well, I hope you all found the tour interesting. If any of you would like to become a patron of the museum, you can request information from the Museum Store. Being a patron entitles you to special discounts on visiting exhibitions and first refusal on tickets to special events. You will also be the first to know about our museum events as you are automatically placed on the museum's mailing list. (16) You can choose to become a 'Gold', 'Silver' or 'Bronze' patron of the museum. 'Gold' patrons are also permitted free entry for one accompanying guest. However, all patrons can receive year-round benefits that are not enjoyed by non-patrons. Having said all that, I would now like to announce some very special news. Next year will be our centenary celebrations. It's hard to believe it, but the museum was founded over 100 years ago! Accordingly, we will be seeing in the New Year in style with a special Masked Ball. This has been organised in response to a special request from some of our patrons. (17) Plans have yet to be finalised for this one-off event, but a 'themed' Masked Ball has been suggested, (18) the idea being that guests come in the guise of famous artists, past or present. One exciting event that has been confirmed is the Summer Garden Party. We are anticipating a lot of interest for this one, so it's best to book well in advance. Whilst the tickets are by no means cheap, we like to think that the price reflects the quality of the event. Amongst the many treats we have in store for you is a live orchestra playing in the museum's gardens, which are to the back of the main building. It is weather-permitting, of course. (19) Again we are dependent on good weather in order for the barbecue to take place. Alternatively, a sit-down meal will be provided in the Cowell Room. Everything from the entertainment to the food is included in the ticket price, so there are no hidden extras!

Now, having given you a round-up of the highlights of next year's social events, let's go on to the artistic highlights of next month. Coming up shortly is Euan Bailey's newest installation, 'Light and Sound Waves'. Always thought-provoking, his previous installations have been very well-received. (20) We will also have Hamish Barnes here for the first time as artist-in-residence. He will be encouraging visitors to adopt a more 'hands-on' approach to art!

Finally, last but not least, we will be exhibiting the work of Sean Long, who will be making his artistic debut. (20) His work will be on show in the Warburton Gallery over the summer period. We are anticipating a large attendance at his exhibition. Well, that's all from me. I look forward to seeing you at one or maybe all of our events. It's certainly going to be an action-packed year for the museum, both culturally and socially!

Narrator: That's the end of Section 2. You have half a minute to check your answers. *[Pause – 30 seconds]*
Now turn to Section 3.

## Section 3

You will hear part of a televised question and answer session between a celebrated art critic and three members of the public, following a talk on 'Outsider Art'. First you have some time to look at questions 21–25. *[Pause – 30 seconds]*
Now listen carefully and answer questions 21–25.

**Art critic:** I think I've said enough, so now it's the turn of the audience. Would anyone like to start the ball rolling and comment on anything I said earlier in my talk? Ah, that young gentleman over there ...

**Audience member 1 (Jake):** Hi. My name's Jake and I've got a question for you. You referred to outsider art as being the work of self-taught, rather than trained or professional artists ... (21) Does that mean anyone can produce art, then?

**Art critic:** Well, what we define as art will always remain subjective. (22) But given that we can agree more or less on a common perception of what is actually 'art', then yes, anyone in theory can produce art. The challenge, though, is to produce 'good art'.

**Audience member 2 (Lucy):** Excuse me. May I ask a question, please?

**Art critic:** Yes, of course. Would you like to introduce yourself to the audience?

**Audience member 2 (Lucy):** Sure, my name's Lucy.

**Art critic:** So Lucy, what would you like to ask?

**Audience member 2 (Lucy):** Don't you think that untrained artists lack the necessary technique to produce good art? I felt that some of the paintings by 'outsider' artists that you showed us earlier were, to be honest, rather crude.

**Art critic:** I think you're confusing technique with art, here. A great technique doesn't guarantee great art, you know. But I think impressive art can still be produced by gifted artists lacking in what are accepted as basic art skills. (23) OK. Can I have another question from a member of the audience, please?

**Audience member 3 (Dave):** Hi. I've got a question. Oh, my name's Dave, by the way, I just wanted to ask how many outsider artists were or are recognised in their lifetime?

**Art critic:** Relatively few. (24) The exceptions are the ones who create particularly monumental or significant works of art, like Nek Chand's sculpture garden in India or Ferdinand Cheval's fantastic building, the 'Palace Ideal'. Both, as you know, were created purely from recycled materials.

**Audience member 3 (Dave):** Yeah, they were pretty amazing. I remember them from the slides you showed earlier.

**Art critic:** But what impresses people most is not so much the sheer scale of these buildings and sculptures, as the work involved. These artists built their works single-handedly over many years and, more to the point, in total secret, as they lacked planning permission. (25) That adds to the romance of the whole undertaking, don't you think?

**Audience member 3 (Dave):** Well, their work certainly impressed me!

**Art critic:** Yes, outsider art certainly produces work that is one-of-a-kind.

Narrator: Before you hear the rest of the discussion, you have some time to look at questions 26–30. *[Pause – 30 seconds]*
Now listen and answer questions 26–30.

**Art critic:** So, now I would like to pose some questions to the audience. First, I would like to ask someone from the audience which, out of all the outsider artwork I showed you previously, is the most impressive and why?

**Audience member 1 (Jake):** Excuse me, may I ...?

**Art critic:** Oh yes, hello again, Jake. So tell me, which artwork was your favourite?

**Audience member 1 (Jake):** Well, funnily enough, the paintings by Adolf Wolfi. I know the perspective is crazy and all over the place, but the work is so detailed!

**Art critic:** Well, look at the great artists, like Picasso and Matisse. Perspective, or lack of it, was never an issue with them.

**Audience member 1 (Jake):** Oddly, whilst I appreciate that style in outsider art, I can't say the same for modern art. I guess it's because I don't approach the two art forms with the same set of expectations.

**Art critic:** Interesting ... You mean you expect more of artists with obvious skill and a professional training, like Picasso and Matisse?

**Audience member 1 (Jake):** Guess so. You know, I expect modern artists to use conventions like perspective, at least. And another thing: I can't really understand why modern artists are often so highly acclaimed by critics (26), whilst outsider artists are virtually ignored – that's probably because they are generally not as skillful, I suppose (27).

**Art critic:** I take your point. I imagine with the exception of outsider artists, you tend to like work by more traditional artists?

**Audience member 1 (Jake):** I suppose. Like everyone, I can appreciate Renaissance Art as exemplified by Da Vinci and Michelangelo. (28) Amazing technique and all that ... and I also understand the popularity of Impressionist artists, too. (29)

**Art critic:** One other question. What's your opinion of modern sculpture? Do you have the same opinion of modern sculpture as you do of modern painting?

**Audience member 1 (Jake):** I think all sculptors have to be pretty skilled to work with materials like metal and stone, so I admire them in a way. But many modern sculptures, particularly public artworks, are often given praise I feel they don't deserve. (30)

**Art critic:** Hmmm ... You seem to have quite definite views about art! Well, it was most interesting hearing your views.

**Narrator:** That's the end of Section 3. You have half a minute to check your answers. *[Pause – 30 seconds]*
Now turn to Section 4.

## Section 4

**You will hear part of an art lecture. First you have some time to look at questions 31–40.** *[Pause – 1 minute]*
**Now listen carefully and answer questions 31–40.**

**Lecturer:** I have just shown you all some slides of a very varied set of paintings. I noticed, as I was showing the slides, a few giggles in the audience and a few looks of dismay. I guess entitling my lecture 'unconventional art geniuses' was a bit misleading. When most of you were looking at the frankly basic colour use (31) and rather primitive painting techniques, you probably were more than a little surprised.

Well, I have a shock for you all. What I'm about to tell you next will help you understand the title of my lecture. All the slides I showed you previously are of artworks made by ... wait for it ... animals! Yes, I heard a few gasps in the audience when I said that. Whilst the artwork would be definitely primitive by human (32) standards, when you consider that the artworks were executed by animals, then, well, they are frankly staggering! Nor were the artworks purely the work of our closest (33) relatives, the apes. No, they were produced by animal artists drawn from a diverse pool of species, ranging from elephants to gorillas, birds and even sloths! In fact, in recognition (34) of this, last year, London's Grant Museum of Zoology staged what organisers thought was the first interspecies show of

paintings by animals. In the show, art was shown from an orangutan, a gorilla and an elephant. Whilst the gorilla and the orangutan produced works that bore a resemblance to the paintings of modern artists de Kooning and Kline, the elephant's (35) work took a more figurative approach in the rendering of a flower pot.

Now before you all go thinking this is a revolutionary discovery, I would like to put the record straight. The contribution animals can make to the art world was highlighted as far back as the 1950s. In this decade, Desmond Morris, celebrated social anthropologist and author of bestsellers such as 'Bodywatching' and 'The Naked Ape', introduced Congo, the painting chimp, to the British public in a TV appearance. Back then, animal art-makers were regarded as little more than a novelty (36). Today, however, animal artists are not viewed so much as novelties but as sophisticated creators with skills and senses that they use to execute artworks in ways humans never can.

As a result of animals being taken more seriously as creators of art, it has become commonplace today for zoos to provide materials to captive animals. The hope is that by giving animals the means to create art, they will be kept physically and mentally stimulated. Obviously you can't give a lizard a paintbrush and expect it to draw! What the zookeepers do, though, is to give animals species-appropriate art materials (37) and tools. For example, sloth bears, who feed by blowing away dirt from the forest floor to feed on termites, have been given a straw-like apparatus to blow paint onto a canvas.

What is one of the most interesting discoveries to come out of all this, though, is the finding that animals voluntarily and instinctively participate in the creation of art. It seems therefore that animals derive as much pleasure as humans do in applying paint to canvas or making a clay or plasticine figure. The obvious conclusion to draw from all this is that there are more similarities (38) between Man and other animals than some of us might care to admit.

However, just to satisfy the sceptics amongst you, there is something I would like to add. So far, the primate and elephant art that has been produced often bears an uncanny resemblance to Western art. Certain conventions are evident in the animals' art that suggests a degree of human intervention (39). As proof of this, an elephant named Boon Mee was actually guided by a keeper who steered the animal's trunk to paint brushstrokes on a canvas! Nevertheless, we should keep an open mind (40) about animal art as there are just as many examples of artworks that have been completed by animals without human aid.

**Narrator:** That is the end of Section 4. You now have half a minute to check your answers. *[Pause – 30 seconds]*
**That is the end of the listening test. You now have 10 minutes to transfer your answers to the Listening Answer Sheet.**

## Test 1

### Task 1 – Model Answer

*This is an example of a very good answer. There are many different approaches that could be taken, however, and this is just one of them.*

From the data in the graph, we can see the effect of a benefit system reform on the amount of incapacity benefit received by older UK men from 1970 to 2015.

The graph shows three age groups. All three groups had a steady rise in incapacity benefits payouts from 1970 to the 1995 reform. The 60–64 age group appears to have the biggest problem with mental health issues at this time.

After the 1995 reform, all three groups take a drop in numbers receiving incapacity benefits, but the 65–69 age group take a staggering drop from 20% to about 2% by 2015. The decrease in the other two age groups is steady but less dramatic. The age group that seems to have been the least affected by the reform is the 55–59 age group, which only had a decrease in benefit receipt of about 6% after the 1995 reform.

We can conclude from the graph that the 1995 reform led to a significant decrease in the amount of incapacity benefits received by older UK men, although the graph does not give us information about why this should be so.

### Task 2 – Model Answer

*This is an example of a very good answer. There are many different approaches that could be taken, however, and this is just one of them.*

I believe it is true to say that there is a difference in attitude towards psychological illness and physical illness. However, there seems to be a shift in attitudes in society as people become more aware of and informed about mental illness.

Firstly, we have to acknowledge that the very fact that psychological illnesses cannot always be seen creates a problem in itself. It is very easy for someone to have serious health problems that other people are unaware of and this, of course, can lead to problems as the person who is ill may behave in an antisocial or unusual way. This can lead to offence and misunderstanding. On the other hand, if someone is physically ill, it is usually clear for all to see and, therefore, people are more likely to be sympathetic and compassionate towards that person.

This leads to the question of how society can change to be more inclusive of those suffering from mental health issues and how they can be helped. In the past, psychological illness was indeed a taboo subject that people felt uncomfortable with. However, this is not so much the case these days due to better awareness and education and an acceptance that anyone can suffer from both mental and physical illness.

I believe that most developed societies are doing their best to tackle this problem. Modern life is incredibly stressful and people are generally under a lot of pressure. Because this affects people from all walks of life, we are all better informed and more tolerant, and I believe that the future will bring more and more help for everyone suffering from psychological problems.

# Test 2

## Task 1 – Model Answer

*This is an example of a very good answer. There are many different approaches that could be taken, however, and this is just one of them.*

From the information in the graph, we can see how different methods of study affect the rate at which a person can learn a language. We are given three different methods of study; studying with a private tutor 1 to 1, in a group at a language school and, finally, self-study.

The difference in results between these three methods is quite dramatic. It is clear that the most effective way to study is through 1 to 1 tuition. The graph shows that with just 50 hours of teaching, a student can go from being a complete beginner to level B2.

The second most effective method is studying in a class at a language school. This would take a student approximately 155 hours to reach the same level. That is nearly three times as long. Finally, self-study would take about 290 hours to reach the B2 level, which is six times as long as 1 to 1 teaching takes.

We can conclude from this data that the fastest way to learn a language is through 1 to 1 tuition, although the other two methods are both effective in the long run.

## Task 2 – Model Answer

*This is an example of a very good answer. There are many different approaches that could be taken, however, and this is just one of them.*

I believe it is quite clear that children's speech develops at different rates. There are many factors that can affect this development, such as having siblings and interacting with other people from a young age. Naturally, every parent wants the best for their child, and some may become over-anxious if they feel that their child's speech is developing more slowly than that of other children. Some may, in fact, turn to speech therapists to speed up their child's development.

The dilemma parents have is whether they should intervene in their child's development or if they should leave the child to develop naturally at their own pace. I believe that if parents have a real concern about their child's speech, it is worth discussing the issue with the school. Teachers have a lot of experience of child development and are well qualified to tell parents if a child has a problem or not.

Some people believe that children should always be allowed to develop at their own pace, but this can create problems if indeed the child does have an issue that they need help with. On the other hand, parents are sometimes too pushy and expect too much too quickly. The answer is a common sense approach to the issue and careful but discreet monitoring of the child's progress.

I personally believe that every child should be able to progress at their own pace, but should be given plenty of opportunities to interact with other people. Parents and professionals must always be aware that there may be issues and keep an open mind as to what the issues are and how they should be dealt with.

# Test 3

### Task 1 – Model Answer

*This is an example of a very good answer. There are many different approaches that could be taken, however, and this is just one of them.*

The data in the bar chart shows how different arts and cultural organisations were affected by taxation last year.

We can clearly see that some organisations are obliged to pay tax, whereas some others do not. The first thing that stands out is that all retail art dealers were liable for tax. This makes sense, as they are set up as businesses for the sole purpose of making money for the owners.

The second biggest taxpayers of the group are the performing arts organisations. About three-quarters of these pay tax. Again, this is most likely due to the fact that many of them charge their audiences and, therefore, are running as a profitable business.

When it comes to museums and historical sites, only a very small proportion pay tax. Presumably, any profit they make through admission fees is ploughed back into the organisation to maintain it.

To sum up, it appears that organisations that are set up to make money as a business pay tax, while those that are of cultural importance and for the benefit of society do not.

### Task 2 – Model Answer

*This is an example of a very good answer. There are many different approaches that could be taken, however, and this is just one of them.*

It has always been the way of the world that very few artists achieve fame through their work, and it has always been a difficult profession to earn a living from. As a result, some people would argue that it is irresponsible for parents to encourage their child to pursue a career in art. This, however, is very much a matter of opinion.

The argument that an artistic career should not be encouraged by parents has its merits. It is obviously safer financially for a child to work towards a career that more or less guarantees a secure wage. Every parent wants their child to do well, and earning decent money is part of that.

I would argue, though, that if a child has a natural leaning towards art and creativity, they should be encouraged. The arts are an essential part of society. It is not all about Fine Art, either. Apart from wanting to see inspiring paintings, sculptures, ceramics, etc., we need designers for many aspects of life. Design includes a whole area of study, from fashion to architecture and technology.

Apart from these things, art offers something that other careers cannot. It gives people a means of expression and builds a cultural heritage that everyone can enjoy, especially those people who do not have artistic talents themselves.

In conclusion, I believe that parents have a duty to encourage any passion and enthusiasm that their child has. They should be on hand to offer advice and guidance, but, ultimately, it should be the individual child who has the final say over which career path they choose to take.

# TEST 1

## READING
### SECTION 1
Questions: 1–8

**1. True.** 'Albert Einstein is perhaps the best-known scientist of the 20th century.', ' … his theories of special and general relativity are of great importance to many branches of physics and astronomy.' **(para. 1)**

**2. True.** 'It is well documented that Einstein did not begin speaking until after the age of three. In fact, he found speaking so difficult that his family were worried that he would never start to speak.' **(para. 3)**

**3. False.** 'It looked as if the needle was moving itself. But the needle was inside a closed case, so no other force (such as the wind) could have been moving it'. **(para. 3)**

**4. False.** 'He finished secondary school in Aarau, Switzerland, and entered the Swiss Federal Institute of Technology in Zurich, from which he graduated in 1900. But Einstein did not like the teaching there either.' **(para. 4)**

**5. Not Given.** 'He often missed classes and used the time to study physics on his own or to play the violin instead.' **(para. 4)** The text doesn't state who taught Einstein to play the violin; it only mentions that he sometimes played the violin when he didn't go to school.

**6. False.** 'His daughter … died at the age of two.' It is generally believed that she died from scarlet fever, but there are those who believe that she may have suffered from a disorder known as Down Syndrome. **(para. 5)**

**7. False.** ' … no one even knew that she had existed until Einstein's granddaughter found 54 love letters that Einstein and Mileva had written to each other between 1897 and 1903. She found these letters inside a shoe box in their attic in California.' **(para. 5)** Einstein and Mileva had written some letters to each other between 1897 and 1903. Einstein's granddaughter found these letters many years later.

**8. Not Given.** ' … in 1933, following death threats from the Nazis, he moved to the United States, where he died on 18th April, 1955.' **(para. 6)** In 1933, Einstein moved to the USA, but the text doesn't state whether he became an American citizen or not.

Questions 9–10

**9. pointed north.** 'He wanted to understand why the needle always *pointed north* whichever way he turned the compass.' **(para. 3)**

**10. on his own.** 'He often missed classes and used the time to study physics *on his own* or to play the violin instead.' **(para. 4)**

Questions 11–13

**11. B.** 'His daughter (whose name we do not know) …' **(para. 5)**

**12. A.** 'His teachers did not have a good opinion of him and refused to recommend him for a university position.' **(para. 4)**

**13. B.** 'Einstein was born in Württemberg, Germany, on 14th March, 1879. His family was Jewish …' **(para. 2)**

## SECTION 2
Questions: 14–20

**14. A.** 'The body is made up mainly of water … Filtered water is healthier than tap water … Substances that settle on the bottom of a glass of tap water and microorganisms … are examples of contaminants. Filtered water is also free of poisonous metals …'

**15. F.** 'There are many different ways to filter water … For example, activated carbon water filters are very good at taking chlorine out. Ozone water filters, on the other hand, are particularly effective at removing germs.'

**16. E.** 'The benefits of water are well known. We all know, for example, that it helps to detoxify the body. So, the purer the water we drink, the easier it is for the body to rid itself of toxins.'

**17. G.** ' … it is very important to know exactly what is in the water that we drink so that we can decide what type of water filter to use.'

**18. C.** 'Scientists believe there could be a connection between mercury in the water and many allergies and cancers, as well as disorders such as ADD, OCD, autism and depression.'

**19. D.** 'Lead … finds its way into our drinking water due to bad pipes. … modern pipes are not made of lead, but pipes in old houses usually are. Lead is a well-known carcinogen …'

**20. B.** 'The authorities know that normal tap water is full of contaminants and they use chemicals, such as chlorine and bromine, in order to disinfect it.'

Questions: 21–26

**21. True.** ' … the quality of water that we drink every day has an important effect on our health.' **(para. A)**

**22. False.** 'Filtered water is typically free of such water disinfectant chemicals. **(para. B)**

**23. True.** 'The authorities … use chemicals such as chlorine and bromine in order to disinfect it (tap water). But such chemicals are hardly safe … For example, consuming bromine for a long time may result in low blood pressure, which may then bring about unsteadiness, dizziness or fainting.' **(para. B)**

**24. False.** ' … normal tap water is full of contaminants' **(para. B)**

**25. Not Given.** 'Filtered water is also free of metals such as mercury and lead. Mercury has ended up in our drinking water mainly because the dental mixtures used by dentists have not been disposed of safely for a long time.' **(para. C)** The text doesn't state anything about people wearing artificial teeth being more likely to be contaminated.

**26. Not Given.** 'Scientists believe there could be a connection between mercury in the water and … depression.' **(para. C)** No connection between depression and dehydration is stated in the text.

## SECTION 3
Questions: 27–34

**27. True.** 'A speech dysfluency is any of various breaks, irregularities or sound-filled pauses that we make when we are speaking, which are commonly known as fillers.' **(para. 1)** 'Fillers … are not generally recognised as meaningful … they can also be used as a pause for thought.' **(para. 2)**

**28. True.** 'Research in linguistics has shown that fillers change across cultures and that even the different English-speaking nations use different fillers.' **(para. 3)**

**29. False.** 'Fillers are normally avoided on television and films, but they occur quite regularly in everyday conversation, sometimes making up more than 20% of "words" in speech.' **(para. 2)**

**30. True.** ' … as Americans get older, they use 'uh' more than 'um' and that men use 'uh' more than women, no matter their age.' **(para. 5)**

**31. Not Given.** 'Spanish speakers say 'ehhh' …' **(para. 3)** The text doesn't state anything about the filler 'ehhh' being used more by younger Spaniards.

**32. False.** '… scientists used to think that fillers had to do more with the amount of time a speaker pauses for, rather than with who the speaker was.' **(para. 5)**

**33. Not Given.** 'Liberman mentioned his finding to fellow linguists in the Netherlands …' **(para. 6)** Nothing is mentioned in the text about Liberman being on a coffee break at the time.

**34. False.** 'sociolinguist Josef Fruehwald may have an answer. In his view, 'um' and 'uh' are pretty much equivalent. The fact that young people and women prefer it is not significant.' **(para. 8)** What he doesn't believe is that it is significant that there are differences between age and gender; he accepts that they exist, though.

**Questions: 35–40**

**35. D.** 'Fillers are normally avoided on television and films …' **(para. 2)**

**36. B.** 'According to the University of Pennsylvania linguist Mark Liberman, 'um' generally comes before a longer or more important pause than 'uh'.' **(para. 4)**

**37. B.** 'Recent linguistic research has suggested that the use of 'uh' and 'um' in English is connected to the speaker's mental and emotional state.' **(para. 4)**

**38. A.** 'What is strange, however, is that 'um' is replacing 'uh' across at least two continents and five Germanic languages. Now this really is a mystery.' **(para. 7)**

**39. D.** 'Women and young people normally are the typical pioneers of most language change.' **(para. 7)**

**40. D.** 'The University of Edinburgh sociolinguist Josef Fruehwald may have an answer. In his view, 'um' and 'uh' are pretty much equivalent. The fact that young people and women prefer it is not significant. This often happens in language when there are two options. People start using one more often until the other is no longer an option.' **(para. 8)**

# TEST 2

**READING**
## SECTION 1
**Questions 1–8**

**1. False.** 'Everyone daydreams sometimes. We sit or lie down, close our eyes and use our imagination to think about something that might happen in the future or could have happened in the past.' **(para. 1)**

**2. False.** 'Daydreams are not dreams, because we can only daydream if we are awake.' **(para. 2)**

**3. True.** '… our daydreams often help us to work out what we want to do, or how to do it to get the best results. So, these daydreams are helpful.' **(para. 2)**

**4. True.** 'Research in the 1980s … showed that over 75% of workers in so-called 'boring jobs', such as lorry drivers and security guards, spend a lot of time daydreaming in order to make their time at work more interesting.' **(para. 4)**

**5. Not Given.** No comparison is made in the text between factory workers and lorry drivers about how often they daydream. 'Research in the 1980s … showed that over 75% of workers in so-called 'boring jobs', such as lorry drivers and security guards, spend a lot of time daydreaming in order to make their time at work more interesting.' **(para. 4)** 'In the 19th century … people who daydreamed a lot were judged

to be lazy. This happened in particular when people started working in factories on assembly lines.' **(para. 5)**

**6. True.** 'Daydreams can help people to be creative.' **(para. 3)**

**7. Not Given.** No comparison is made in the text between old and young people. 'Everyone daydreams sometimes.' **(para. 1)**

**8. False.** 'Escapist people spend a lot of time living in a dream world in which they are successful and popular … Such people often seem to be unhappy and are unable or unwilling to improve their daily lives.' **(para. 6)**

**Questions: 9–10**

**9. develop new ideas.** 'People in creative or artistic careers, such as composers, novelists and filmmakers, *develop new ideas* through daydreaming.' **(para. 3)**

**10. problem-solving.** 'Experiments with MRI brain scans show that the parts of the brain linked with complex *problem-solving* are more active during daydreaming.' **(para. 4)**

**Questions 11–13**

**11. C.** 'We … think about something that might happen in the future or could have happened in the past. Most daydreaming is pleasant … We might daydream that we are in another person's place, or doing something that we have always wanted to do, or that other people like or admire us much more than they normally do.' **(para. 1)**

**12. B.** 'In the 19th century, for example, people who daydreamed a lot were judged to be lazy.' **(para. 5)**

**13. D.** '… recent studies show that people who often daydream have fewer close friends than other people. In fact, they often do not have any close friends at all.' **(para. 6)**

## SECTION 2
**Questions: 14–19**

**14. C.** 'In 1820 in his book *The Philosophy of Arithmetic*, the mathematician John Leslie recommended that young pupils memorise the times tables up to 25×25.'

**15. F.** 'Research has shown that learning and remembering sums involving 6, 7, 8 and 9 tends to be harder than remembering sums involving other numbers … Studies often find that the hardest sum is 6×8, with 7×8 not far behind. However, even though 7×8 is a relatively difficult sum …'

**16. G.** 'It is well known that when there is a lot of pressure to do something right, people often have difficulty doing something that they normally find easy.'

**17. A.** 'Children have traditionally learned their times tables by going from '1 times 1 is 1' all the way up to '12 times 12 is 144'.'

**18. D.** 'For example, in 1998, the schools minister Stephen Byers was asked the answer to 7×8. He got the answer wrong, saying 54 rather than 56, and everyone laughed at him.'

**19. B.** 'The oldest known tables using base 10 numbers … are written on bamboo strips dating from 305 BC found in China. However, in many European cultures the times tables are named after the Ancient Greek mathematician and philosopher Pythagoras (570–495 BC).'

**Questions: 20–25**

**20. False.** 'The oldest known tables using base 10 numbers are … found in China. However, in many European cultures the times tables are named after the Ancient Greek mathematician and philosopher Pythagoras (570–495 BC).' **(para. B)**

**21. True.** '... the schools minister Stephen Byers was asked the answer to 7×8.' **(para. D)** 'In 2014, a young boy asked the UK Chancellor George Osborne the exact same question.' **(para. E)**

**22. True.** 'The current aim in the UK is for school pupils to know all their times tables up to 12×12 by the age of nine.' **(para. D)**

**23. False.** '... even though 7×8 is a relatively difficult sum, it is highly unlikely that George Osborne did not know the answer. So there must be some other reason why he refused to answer the question.' **(para. F)**

**24. False.** 'Studies often find that the hardest sum is 6×8, with 7×8 not far behind.' **(para. F)**

**25. Not Given.** 'For example, in 1998, the schools minister Stephen Byers was asked the answer to 7×8.' **(para. D)** There is no mention of how long Stephen Byers had been the schools minister.

## SECTION 3
**Questions: 26–31**

**26. D.** 'In popular literature of the Victorian era which reflected true-life events, individuals were frequently sent to the 'madhouse' as a legal means of permanently disposing of an unwanted heir or spouse.' **(para. 2)**

**27. B.** 'Patient 'treatment' amounted to little more than legitimised abuse. Inmates were beaten and forced to live in unsanitary conditions, whilst others were placed on display to a curious public as a sideshow.' **(para. 1)** 'Even up until the mid-20th century, institutions for the mentally ill were regarded as being more places of isolation and punishment than healing and solace.' **(para. 2)**

**28. B.** 'Little wonder then that the appalling catalogue of treatment of the mentally ill led to a call for change from social activists and psychologists alike.' **(para. 2)**

**29. A.** 'In its early stages, however, community care consisted primarily of help from the patient's extended family network. In more recent years, such care has been extended to the provision of specialist community mental health teams ...' **(para. 3)**

**30. B.** 'In more recent years, such care has been extended to the provision of specialist community mental health teams (CMHTs) in the UK. Such teams cover a wide range of services, from rehabilitation to home treatment and assessment. In addition, psychiatric nurses are on hand to administer prescription medication and give injections.' **(para. 3)**

**31. B.** 'Often, though, when a policy is put into practice, its failings become apparent. This is true for the policy of care in the community.', 'The solution, therefore, is to ensure that the patient is always in touch with professional helpers and not left alone to fend for themselves. It should always be remembered that whilst you can take the patient out of the institution, you can't take the institution out of the patient.' **(para. 4)**

**Questions: 32–36**

**32. A.** 'Dr Mayalla ... is inclined to believe that ... 'Those suffering moderate cases of mental illness stand to gain more from care in the community than those with more pronounced mental illness. I don't think it's a one-size-fits-all policy. But I also think that there is a far better infrastructure of helpers and social workers in place now than previously, and the scheme stands a greater chance of success than in the past.'' **(para. 5)**

**33. C.** 'Bob Ratchett ... takes a more positive view of community care projects. 'Having worked in the field myself, I've seen how a patient can benefit from living an independent life, away from an institution. If you think about it, is it really fair to condemn an individual to a lifetime in an institution when they could be living a fairly fulfilled and independent life outside the institution?' **(para. 7)**

**34. C.** 'Bob Ratchett ... takes a more positive view of community care projects. 'Having worked in the field myself, I've seen how a patient can benefit from living an independent life, away from an institution.' **(para. 7)**

**35. B.** 'Anita Brown ... takes a different view.' ... I would not put my support behind any scheme that I felt might put my children in danger ... I like to feel secure where I live, but more to the point, that my children are not under any threat.' **(para. 6)**

**36. B.** 'Anita Brown ... takes a different view ... I guess there must be assessment methods in place to ensure that dangerous individuals are not let loose amongst the public, but I'm not for it at all.' **(para. 6)**

**Questions: 37–40**

**37. Not Given.** There is no specific mention of helping children with mental health issues.

**38. False.** 'In more recent years ... Such teams cover a wide range of services, from rehabilitation to home treatment and assessment. In addition, psychiatric nurses are on hand to administer prescription medication and give injections. The patient is therefore provided with the necessary help that they need to survive in the everyday world whilst maintaining a degree of autonomy.' **(para. 3)**

**39. False.** 'Dr Mayalla ... is inclined to believe ... there is a far better infrastructure of helpers and social workers in place now than previously, and the scheme stands a greater chance of success than in the past.' **(para. 5)**

**40. True.** 'In more recent years, such care has been extended to the provision of specialist community mental health teams (CMHTs) in the UK ... The patient is therefore provided with the necessary help that they need to survive in the everyday world whilst maintaining a degree of autonomy.' **(para. 3)**

# TEST 3

**READING**

## SECTION 1
**Questions 1–10**

**1, 2: A/D.**

**A:** 'As the celebrated philosopher, Kant, stated: 'At its best, art cultivates and expands the human spirit', 'The goal of all artists nevertheless, remains the same: to produce a work that simultaneously transcends the mundane and uplifts the viewer.' **(para. 3)**

**D:** 'Art, on the other hand, is not restricted by the confines of practicality.', 'In fact, the very reason for art and its existence is purely to 'be' ...' **(para. 2)**, 'Artistic products appeal purely at the level of the imagination.' **(para. 3)**

**3, 4, 5: F/G/J.**

**F:** 'The artist is ... just as unaware as anyone else as to what the end product of creation will be when he is actually in the process of creating.' **(para. 4)**, 'The artist is at the mercy of inspiration alone and ... may never be able to guarantee that the object will be finished at all. Unfinished symphonies by great composers and works of literature never completed by their authors testify to this.' **(para. 5)**

G: 'Since the artist is not following a set of standard rules in the process of creation ...', 'For it is the artist alone who, through a trial-and-error approach, will create the final object.' **(para. 5)**

J: 'Art is placed by Collingwood at the other end of the creative continuum, the creation of art being described as a process that evolves non-deterministically.' **(para. 4)**, 'The artist is at the mercy of inspiration alone and, quite apart from not being able to have a projected finishing date, may never be able to guarantee that the object will be finished at all.' **(para. 5)**

**6, 7: B/C.**

B: 'The craftsman's teapot or vase should normally be able to hold tea or flowers ...' **(para. 2)**, '... the world of the craftsman and his work remain lodged firmly in the practicality of the everyday world.' **(para. 3)**

C: '... the concept of craft is historically associated with the production of useful or practical products.' **(para. 2)**, 'Artistry in craftsmanship is therefore merely a by-product, since the primary focus is on what something does, not what it is.' **(para. 3)**

**8, 9, 10: E/H/I.**

E: 'With a craft, Collingwood argued, the 'result to be obtained is preconceived or thought out before being arrived at'. **(para. 4)**

H: 'The craftsman, Collingwood says, 'knows what he wants to make before he makes it'. This foreknowledge, according to Collingwood, must not be vague, but precise. In fact, such planning is considered to be 'indispensable' to craft.' **(para. 4)**, 'the table or chair created by the craftsman, for example, has to conform to certain expectations in appearance and design ...', '... the craftsman can fairly accurately predict when a product will be finished, taking technical procedures into account ...' **(para. 5)**

I: 'With a craft, Collingwood argued, the 'result to be obtained is preconceived or thought out before being arrived at'. The craftsman, Collingwood says, 'knows what he wants to make before he makes it'.' **(para. 4)**

# SECTION 2
## Questions: 11–13

11. C. 'He was only 14 when his first works were exhibited as part of a show in Figueres.', '... the rebellious artist left for Paris. There, he hoped to avail himself of knowledge that he believed his tutors were not adequate to impart.' **(para. 3)**

12. E. 'Already familiar with the psychoanalytic theories of Sigmund Freud, Dali was to witness how the French Surrealists were attempting to capture Freud's ideas in paint. The whole world of the unconscious sublimated into dreams was to become the content of these artists' work and later that of Dali's, too.' **(para. 4)**

13. D. 'Despite a lukewarm reception from critics, Dali's public popularity never declined. In 1974, at 70 years old, the Dali Theatre Museum opened in his hometown, Figueres ... even today, hundreds of thousands of visitors still tour the museum each year. Whatever your opinion of him, at least Dali is unlikely to ever be forgotten.' **(para. 8)**

## Questions: 14–16

14. D. 'Believing himself way superior to the Academy tutors, who refused to grant him a degree, the rebellious artist left for Paris. There, he hoped to avail himself of knowledge that he believed his tutors were not adequate to impart.' **(para. 3)**

15. B. '... Dali's work has achieved enduring worldwide fame as his name and work have become virtually synonymous with Surrealism itself. The artist's melting clock image is surely one of the most iconic paintings of the art world, whilst Dali's antics have become the stuff of anecdote.' **(para. 1)**

16. B. 'Dali's Surrealist paintings were packed with Freudian imagery: staircases, keys, dripping candles, in addition to a whole host of personally relevant symbolism, such as grasshoppers and ants, that captured his phobias on canvas.' **(para. 5)**

## Questions: 17–18
**17, 18: C, D.**

C: 'Few with even a passing knowledge of the art world are likely not to have heard of Salvador Dali, the eccentric and avant-garde exponent of the Surrealist movement.' **(para. 1)**

D: '... Dali's work has achieved enduring worldwide fame as his name and work have become virtually synonymous with Surrealism itself. The artist's melting clock image is surely one of the most iconic paintings of the art world, whilst Dali's antics have become the stuff of anecdote.' **(para. 1)**

## Questions: 19–21

19. C. 'He was only 14 when his first works were exhibited as part of a show in Figueres. Then, three years later, he was admitted to the Royal Academy of Fine Arts ... it wasn't long before Dali's highly developed sense of self-worth (or conceit, depending on how you view the artist) came to the fore and also affected the course of his life. Believing himself way superior to the Academy tutors ... left for Paris. There, he hoped to avail himself of knowledge that he believed his tutors were not adequate to impart.' **(para. 3)**

20. C. 'His critics ... believed that early on in his career his love of money exceeded his dedication to producing great art, resulting in Dali producing 'awful junk' after 1939, according to one art critic.' **(para. 7)**

21. D. 'Despite a lukewarm reception from critics, Dali's public popularity never declined. In 1974, at 70 years old, the Dali Theatre Museum opened in his hometown, Figueres ... even today, hundreds of thousands of visitors still tour the museum each year. Whatever your opinion of him, at least Dali is unlikely to ever be forgotten.' **(para. 8)**

## Questions: 22–26

22. worldwide fame. 'Dali's work has achieved enduring *worldwide fame* as his name and work have become virtually synonymous with Surrealism itself.' **(para. 1)**

23. ambition/self-belief. 'Such *ambition* and *self-belief* matured into full-blown arrogance in later years.' **(para. 2)**

24. turning point. 'the rebellious artist left for Paris ... He soon made the acquaintance of the French surrealists Jean Arp, Rene Magritte and Max Ernst, and this would prove a *turning point* in Dali's artistic life.' **(para. 3)**

25. psychoanalytic. 'Already familiar with the *psychoanalytic* theories of Sigmund Freud, Dali was to witness how the French Surrealists were attempting to capture Freud's ideas in paint.' **(para. 4)**

## Answer Explanations for the Reading Sections

**26. be forgotten.** 'Whatever your opinion of him, at least Dali is unlikely to ever **be forgotten**.' **(para. 8)**

## SECTION 3
### Questions: 27–32

**27. D.** 'Hiring a driverless cab means that the client does not have to pay for the cost of the driver in the cab fee. The only cost incurred by clients is for fuel, plus wear and tear. It is certainly an attractive proposition. Uber stands to benefit, too, since employees currently working as taxi drivers will be removed from the company's payroll. Apparently, for car drivers and Uber, it is a win-win situation.' **(para. 2)**

**28. A.** 'Whether Uber is backing a doomed campaign or instead is about to bring in a technology that will be universally greeted with positivity and acceptance depends entirely on your viewpoint.' **(para. 6)**, 'John Reynolds, a Pittsburgh taxi driver, is angry at Uber's attitude on fully automated technology.' **(para. 7)**, 'Susie Greenacre, a resident of Pittsburgh, has no such reservations about driverless cars. 'I'm all for it.'' **(para. 8)**, 'Jason Steiner, a school teacher in a secondary school, is inclined to agree with Susie.' **(para. 9)**

**29. A.** 'It seems that even Uber is less than confident that driverless taxis will soon become a reality.' **(para. 6)**

**30. B.** 'Whilst a fully automated car could respond to most eventualities in the course of a trip, would it be capable of responding to unforeseen events, such as changes in route or unexpected diversions? Evidently, legislative authorities are also of this opinion.' **(para. 4)**

**31. C.** 'Not everyone will benefit, however, from this technology, the car industry being an obvious example … the industry views the concept of self-driving cars with a sense of growing alarm. Such technology could well prove the death knell for private car ownership.' **(para. 3)**

**32. B.** 'It seems that even Uber is less than confident that driverless taxis will soon become a reality. Whether Uber is backing a doomed campaign or instead is about to bring in a technology that will be universally greeted with positivity and acceptance depends entirely on your viewpoint.' **(para. 6)**

### Questions: 33–37

**33. C.** 'Jason Steiner … is inclined to agree with Susie. 'Whilst I'm not averse to driving, I would swap the stressful daily commute by car to a driverless one … I would be slightly wary, though, of being completely dependent on a robot-driven car when it comes to having to react to unexpected obstacles in the road'.' **(para. 9)**

**34. B.** 'Susie Greenacre … has no such reservations about driverless cars. 'I'm all for it … I think if I could just hop in a driverless car which would take me anywhere I wanted, I would never want to drive again!'' **(para. 8)**

**35. C.** 'Jason Steiner … I would be slightly wary, though, of being completely dependent on a robot-driven car when it comes to having to react to unexpected obstacles in the road.' **(para. 9)**

**36. A.** 'John Reynolds … Admittedly, things change and we have to roll with the times, but there should be some safeguards in place to protect those potentially affected by the introduction of new technologies.' **(para. 7)**

**37. C.** 'Jason Steiner … Whilst I'm not averse to driving, I would swap the stressful daily commute by car to a driverless one if I had the chance! It just takes the pressure off driving.' **(para. 9)**

### Questions: 38–40

**38. True.** '… there is also the safety issue. Whilst a fully automated car could respond to most eventualities in the course of a trip, would it be capable of responding to unforeseen events, such as changes in route or unexpected diversions? Evidently, legislative authorities are also of this opinion.' **(para. 4)**

**39. False.** 'It seems that even Uber is less than confident that driverless taxis will soon become a reality.' **(para. 6)**

**40. Not Given.** Efforts have been made so that safety issues about driveless cars can be solved, but a time frame isn't stated in the text regarding when this will happen. 'Currently, Uber is … launching the Uber Advanced Technologies Centre in Pittsburgh. The ultimate goal of this institution is to 'do research and development, primarily in the areas of mapping and vehicle safety and autonomy technology.' **(para. 1)**

Answer Key

# TEST 1

**Listening – Section 1**
1. 80 2. limit 3. 4.5 (metres) 4. hire and installation
5. (cost of) carpeting 6. £55 7. June 5th 8. Jenny Lakewell
9. CV6 TL3 10. 07944 325883

**Listening – Section 2**
11.G 12.D 13.C 14.A 15.F 16.B 17.B 18.C 19.A 20.C

**Listening – Section 3**
21.B 22.C 23.C 24.B 25.A 26.A 27.B 28.C 29.B 30.C

**Listening – Section 4**
31. natural world 32. identical theory 33. sole credit
34. controversial 35. of evolution 36. missing link
37. proof of 38. so convincing 39. a fake 40. still remain

**Reading – Section 1**
1.T 2.T 3.F 4.F 5.NG 6.F 7.F 8.NG
9. pointed north 10. on his own 11.B 12.A 13.B

**Reading – Section 2**
14.A 15.F 16.E 17.G 18.C 19.D 20.B 21.T 22.F 23.T 24.F 25.NG
26.NG

**Reading – Section 3**
27.T 28.T 29.F 30.T 31.NG 32.F 33.NG 34.F 35.D 36.B 37.B 38.A
39.D 40.D

# TEST 2

**Listening – Section 1**
1. continental 2. buffet dinner 3. Common
4. booked online 5. all meals 6. lounge 7. Maple View
8. pedestrian 9. bank holidays 10. in advance

**Listening – Section 2**
11.G 12.H 13.E 14.F 15.C 16.B 17.B 18.A 19.C 20.C

**Listening – Section 3**
21.A 22/23. B/E (in any order) 24/25. A/B (in any order)
26.C 27.B 28.A 29.A 30.C

**Listening – Section 4**
31. everyday lives 32. cooperate with 33. handwriting
34. zero 35. mental health 36. cultural 37. coloured cards 38.
convincing tool 39. of people 40. lack

**Reading – Section 1**
1.F 2.F 3.T 4.T 5.NG 6.T 7.NG 8.F
9. develop new ideas 10. problem-solving 11.C 12.B 13.D

**Reading – Section 2**
14.C 15.F 16.G 17.A 18.D 19.B 20.F 21.T 22.T 23.F 24.F 25.NG

**Reading – Section 3**
26.D 27.B 28.B 29.A 30.B 31.B 32.A 33.C 34.C 35.B 36.B 37.NG
38.F 39.F 40.T

# TEST 3

**Listening – Section 1**
1. £300 2. P.J. Browning 3. £500 4. 17th/seventeenth century 5.
English 6. 1.5 metres 7. height 8. Bradwell-Thompson 9. KN26
56T 10. 23rd (of) March

**Listening – Section 2**
11.E 12.F 13.G 14.A 15.B 16.A 17.C 18.A 19.B 20.C

**Listening – Section 3**
21.A 22.A 23.A 24.B 25.B 26.A 27.B 28.C 29.C 30.A

**Listening – Section 4**
31. colour use 32. human 33. closest 34. recognition
35. elephant's 36. novelty 37. Art materials
38. more similarities 39. intervention 40. open mind

**Reading – Section 1**
1.A/D 2.A/D 3.F/G/J 4.F/G/J 5.F/G/J 6.B/C 7.B/C 8.E/H/I 9.E/H/I
10.E/H/I

**Reading – Section 2**
11.C 12.E 13.D 14.D 15.B 16.B 17/18. C/D (in any order)
19.C 20.C 21.D 22. worldwide fame 23. ambition/self-belief
24. turning point 25. psychoanalytic 26. be forgotten

**Reading – Section 3**
27.D 28.A 29.A 30.B 31.C 32.B 33.C 34.B 35.C
36.A 37.C 38.T 39.F 40.NG

# LISTENING TEST ANSWER SHEET

You may **photocopy or reproduce** this page.

⟶ **TRANSFER** your answers from the Listening question pages to this Answer Sheet at the end of the Listening Test. Use one Answer Sheet for each Practice Listening Test.

| | |
|---|---|
| 1 _____ | 21 _____ |
| 2 _____ | 22 _____ |
| 3 _____ | 23 _____ |
| 4 _____ | 24 _____ |
| 5 _____ | 25 _____ |
| 6 _____ | 26 _____ |
| 7 _____ | 27 _____ |
| 8 _____ | 28 _____ |
| 1 _____ | 29 _____ |
| 10 _____ | 30 _____ |
| 11 _____ | 31 _____ |
| 12 _____ | 32 _____ |
| 13 _____ | 33 _____ |
| 14 _____ | 34 _____ |
| 15 _____ | 35 _____ |
| 16 _____ | 36 _____ |
| 17 _____ | 37 _____ |
| 18 _____ | 38 _____ |
| 19 _____ | 39 _____ |
| 20 _____ | 40 _____ |

**Listening TOTAL** _____

# READING TEST ANSWER SHEET

PRACTICE READING TEST

You may **photocopy or reproduce** this page.

⟶ **Use** one Answer Sheet for each Practice Listening Test.

| | |
|---|---|
| 1 _____ | 21 _____ |
| 2 _____ | 22 _____ |
| 3 _____ | 23 _____ |
| 4 _____ | 24 _____ |
| 5 _____ | 25 _____ |
| 6 _____ | 26 _____ |
| 7 _____ | 27 _____ |
| 8 _____ | 28 _____ |
| 1 _____ | 29 _____ |
| 10 _____ | 30 _____ |
| 11 _____ | 31 _____ |
| 12 _____ | 32 _____ |
| 13 _____ | 33 _____ |
| 14 _____ | 34 _____ |
| 15 _____ | 35 _____ |
| 16 _____ | 36 _____ |
| 17 _____ | 37 _____ |
| 18 _____ | 38 _____ |
| 19 _____ | 39 _____ |
| 20 _____ | 40 _____ |

**Reading TOTAL** _____